Further Scrapings
More Musical Memories

by

Peter Mountain

AuthorHouse™ UK Ltd.
500 Avebury Boulevard
Central Milton Keynes, MK9 2BE
www.authorhouse.co.uk
Phone: 08001974150

© 2008 Peter Mountain. All rights reserved.

No part of this book may be reproduced, stored in a retrieval system, or transmitted by any means without the written permission of the author.

First published by AuthorHouse 7/22/2008

ISBN: 978-1-4343-8111-8 (sc)

Printed in the United States of America
Bloomington, Indiana

This book is printed on acid-free paper.

Dedication

To my Family: sister Kath, Paul, Alison, Jeanette, eight Grandchildren, two Great Grandchildren, who conspire together to make my retirement very happy

Also in memory of Muriel (Angela Dale), my wife and lifetime colleague in music, who I shall never forget.

FURTHER SCRAPINGS by PETER MOUNTAIN

More Memories Of A Violinist

Peter Mountain – violinist and author of "Scraping a Living" presents a follow-up volume – "Further Scrapings", in which he digs deeper into his memories of a long life as a musician. He recalls his early days, eighty years ago, when the social scene of his beloved Yorkshire and the world at large were both very different.

There are chapters about early family life, with revealing anecdotes, especially those concerning his strong-minded father who was a great influence. Accounts of school days and local Yorkshire musical activities are entertainingly revealed against a background of the pre-war tension in the nineteen thirties.

The narrative continues on to student life in wartime London, service and travels in Europe and the Far East with the Royal Marine Band, and subsequently establishing a career in post-war London as a member of the Boyd Neel Orchestra and the Philharmonia. Many new anecdotes come to light as he remembers the free-lance scene of that period.

In 1955, he left London to become leader of the Royal Liverpool Philharmonic Orchestra for the next eleven years. After two years back in London, in 1967 he moved to Bristol where he spent the next eight years as Concertmaster of the BBC Training Orchestra, later renamed The Academy of the BBC.

The narrative of this volume ends there, but there are other chapters and appendices which continue up to today, including his ideas on Conducting, Orchestral Leading, Teaching, Money, Motor Cars and Dogs, inviting the reader to share a gift for which he is eternally grateful; a full and varied life.

Contents

Dedication v
Introduction xi

PART I

Chapter 1 - Early Days 2
Chapter 2 - Bradford Musical Life 18
Chapter 3 - Bingley Grammar School 26
Chapter 4 - Harry Mountain 33
Chapter 5 - Music in Schooldays 44
Chapter 6 – Random Memories 48

PART II

Chapter 7 - Student Days 66
Chapter 8 – Marlborough Place 77
Chapter 9 – The War 90
Chapter 10 – The Royal Marines Band, Plymouth Division 94
Chapter 11 – London 1948 to 1955 99
Chapter 12 – Cars 103
Chapter 13 – A Time of Change 110
Chapter 14 – Scraping a Living – The Freelance Scene 117
Chapter 15 – Money Matters 125
Chapter 16 – Leading 131
Chapter 17 – Some Past Notable Orchestral Leaders 140

PART III

Chapter 18 – A New Beginning 166
Chapter 19 – Dogs 169
Chapter 20 – Some Thoughts on Conducting 179
Chapter 21 – Conductors in Liverpool 184
Chapter 22 – Bristol 190
Chapter 23 – Conductors in Bristol 193
Appendix I 200
Appendix II – 213
Index 221
(Footnotes) 227

Introduction

I was born a Yorkshireman and have remained proud to be one ever since. The accent has stayed – more pronounced in times of stress but never completely absent. The legacy of my first 17 years in God's Own County, particularly what used to be the West Riding part of it, has never left me, and having had a sort of *da capo* stay of fifteen years from 1990 to 2004 back in the same area it never will. My present (hopefully extended!) coda section of life's symphony, in the pleasant North Derbyshire town of Glossop, is not too much of a change and gives me a chance to have a detached view of things over the various sections of these memories.

The following chapters are an amplification and continuation of my first book "Scraping a Living"; memories of a career as a typical British violinist in the latter part of the 20th century. In this sequel, I plan to cover some of the many details that I have since recalled and regretfully did not remember earlier. Pictures come flooding back later in life, and I am now revisiting those far off early days in more detail, showing how much, and in some ways how little things have changed.

I have been lucky to have had a varied life and career, that seems to divide itself naturally into six parts – I Yorkshire 17 years, II London 15 years, III Liverpool 11 years, IV London and Bristol 9 years, V Scotland 15 years, and VI Return to Yorkshire 14 years. After that has come final retirement in Glossop. This volume covers the first four parts.

The earliest period of life is certainly very important, as character and habits are formed that consciously or unconsciously direct one through later life. So, let me now think a little of the general background, both social and musical, that I was born into, in the small Yorkshire town of Shipley, on October 3rd 1923.

PART I

1923 TO 1940

YORKSHIRE

Chapter 1 - Early Days

In the year of my birth, the Great War of 1914 to 1918 was a relatively recent happening. I was in a similar position *vis-a-vis* that conflict to someone born in the early 1950's in relation to the second great world upheaval.

In both cases, Britain was only just recovering from wartime hardships and travail.

The young people, the arts and music were forging ahead, creating the freedom and liveliness of both the Gay Twenties (and in the latter case the Swinging Sixties). But when I came into this world the pace of change was slower than in the more recent post-war era, and with the older generation Edwardian and even Victorian ideas still prevailed. My parents were quite open to progressive thinking, but the environment and the ideas of many of their contemporaries were still pretty old fashioned. The dress of both men and women was not dissimilar from Edwardian attire, but within ten or fifteen years it would all change radically; everything pointing to the fact that new ideas were in the air, and slowly but surely different times were coming.

Actual events in 1923 (although I was then blissfully unaware of them) were pointing ahead to a more threatening future. Adolf Hitler, hoping to imitate Mussolini's March on Rome the previous year, led an unsuccessful bid for power in Munich, and was imprisoned. The German Mark plummeted to 42 million to the US Dollar. The following year Lenin died and shortly after Stalin emerged as the Russian ruler. It was the beginning of the era of the Great Dictators.

In the musical world, the Austrian composer Arnold Schoenberg, already notorious as an extreme modernist for his "Erwartung" (1909) and "Five Orchestral Pieces" (1910), took a giant step forward. After the war he had evolved a musical system which he claimed would enable his textures to become simpler and clearer. This resulted in the "method of composition with twelve tones" in which the twelve

Further Scrapings

pitches of the octave are regarded as equal, and no one note or tonality is given the status it has in diatonic harmony. He regarded this as the equivalent in music of Albert Einstein's discoveries in Physics. Schoenberg announced his system characteristically, during a walk with his friend Josef Rufer,[1] when he said "I have today made a discovery which will ensure the supremacy of German music for the next hundred years" This was first employed in his "Serenade" for chamber ensemble which was premiered in 1923.

I must admit frankly that I have never been able to come to terms with twelve tone music. I don't mind dissonance and tonal experiments of many kinds, but I am uncomfortable with the rootless feeling of music having no tonal centre. The idea of making all notes equal seems to me to be artificial. The drama and spirit of musical melody and harmony is based, I think, on the varying significance of each character in the octave scale. You can change the actual key and relish the contrasts this reveals, but to have all notes equal in significance seems essentially monotonous. If you have an ear which remembers the actual sound of notes, generally known as perfect pitch, it is disturbing to swim in a sea of music without the shoreline of a tonic to relate to. Schoenberg certainly had genius and inspired other gifted musicians such as Alban Berg and Anton von Webern, both of whom I admire, but there were other less inspired writers who latched on to this new system and produced what seem to me musical horrors! Thank goodness we now see, well before Schoenberg's hundred years has elapsed, that the supremacy of this system is waning fast. It occurs to me that my lifetime has seen the birth and death of the dodecaphonic system[2] in music almost exactly together with the birth and death of another movement which strove for equality; Russian communism. Perhaps this teaches us that mankind does not take easily to artificially imposed systems, however attractive in theory. Imagine a world where everyone was equal, we played only 12 tone music, and we all spoke Esperanto!

Another musical first performance that took place in New York that year was of George Gershwin's "Rhapsody in Blue". This I love, though I don't think it is the finest of his works – it is just the best known. Gershwin was one of the most spontaneous and prolific composers of the last century - attractive and original music sprang from him in a never ending stream, like a latter day Schubert. The story is told that he took a ride in a New York taxi with his agent. When they got out, the agent suddenly cried – "Oh my God, I've left my briefcase in the taxi, and it had the manuscript of the Twelve Preludes for piano that you've just written! No other copies exist". "Never mind" said Gershwin. "It doesn't matter. I can easily write twelve more!"

So that is one good musical thing coinciding with my birth – the only one of major importance I can track down. On a rather more utilitarian level, you might like to note that 1923 marked the invention of the zip fastener!

But I must return to the narrative.

My mother, Dorothy Wood, was an accomplished pianist, though at that time not a professional player. She was the youngest of her family, with three older brothers, all of whom had returned from the War to marry, leaving her at home to look after her widowed father. (She had a twin sister, who had sadly died, together with her mother, in the 1919 'flu epidemic) The father (my grandfather) was Benjamin Wood, a staid and respectable retired Bradford businessman, a pillar of the nearby Frizinghall Wesleyan Methodist Chapel, and whom I always remember as an old man. A bald pate surrounded by white hair, a grey moustache, slow moving and ponderous, I felt sure he had been born an old man – it was his destiny. He was old even when in his fifties, and he was typically Victorian.

Harry Mountain, a proficient amateur violinist from nearby Bingley, came to woo Dorothy, drawn by their mutual love of music. He had not fought in the War, being rejected by the army because of a perforated eardrum, and I always felt that the Wood brothers (my uncles) held him in slight disdain because of this, and also because of his artistic leanings. He was always regarded in the Wood family as a bit of an eccentric, which accusation in all fairness could not be entirely denied. He was a man of boundless enthusiasm for a great number of other things apart from music, his main love, and he also had an irresistible desire to convert everyone else to his own enthusiasms. That made him a fascinating person to be with for a short time, but he could become a bit wearing in large doses! He and Dorothy were a prime example of the attraction of opposites.

When they married in 1922, Grandpa could not be left alone in the big house and would not consider moving, so they had to set up their home in the very aptly named "Victoria Grove", which is where I was born (literally); where my Mum could look after Grandpa as well as her family, and where I grew up, joined three and a half years later by my sister Kathleen.

Victoria Grove was (and still is) a terrace of three quite spacious houses, set back from the main Bradford Road in Shipley, and had been built by Grandpa, who brought up his family in one of them and sold the other two. The house was very pleasant, with a conservatory at the side, a communal yard at the back, and outhouses with a stable and a coach-house, backed by a long garden. I can clearly remember when Grandpa used to sally forth on excursions with the horse and trap. I believe he regularly ventured as far as Morecambe for family holidays but that must have been when I was very tiny. The coaching days were soon to end when Dad arrived with his Standard motorcar, and the coach house became a garage.

It was decided, unwisely, that I should be born at home. The actual birth was much delayed, and I arrived into this world weighing just over 13 lbs! How my poor Mum must have suffered! Angelically natured as she was, she never seemed to hold it against me. I heard that the doctor first put me aside as being beyond hope of recovery, and it was my paternal Grandma, staying awake for practically an entire fortnight to look after my wounds, who really saved my life. Grandma Mountain was a remarkable lady, and I have written much about her previously.

Grandpa Wood, although retired from business and a semi invalid, strongly retained his status as head of the family. His sons, Stanley and another Benjamin, although having set up house quite nearby, still looked upon Victoria Grove as their ancestral home. Lesley, the third brother, emigrated to Australia, and the last I saw of him was when I was six, but the other two, with their families, always descended on our house for regular family reunions. Chief of these were 5th November – Gunpowder Plot Night – and of course Christmas Day, when the house was filled to capacity and Mum had her hands full providing refreshments for what I remember as a vast multitude.

Plot Night in particular was a traditional never-varying routine. The previous weeks were spent "progging", which meant scouring the neighbourhood for tree branches and any other fuel for the bonfire, built in the back yard on the day. There was always a gargantuan high tea in the house for the whole family. The traditional dish always consumed in large quantities was parkin, a kind of oatmeal, treacle and gingerbread cake – a typical Yorkshire delicacy. Then the fire in the back yard, with the Guy, potatoes and chestnuts baked in the embers, and all our friends from the immediate neighbourhood, letting off the fireworks which had been bought in garishly decorated boxes with pocket-money, saved up for weeks.

Christmas was similarly a big family celebration. We went to chapel in the morning, as long as Grandpa was alive and active, but the Mountain family gradually neglected religious observances. The Woods continued chapel attendance however, so we had our Christmas lunches separately, and the complete family assembled in the afternoon and evening for presents, party games, carol singing and a large meal. During this, Grandpa solemnly produced a bottle of claret that was carefully poured out in small glassfuls for the adults. That was the only time in the year that alcoholic beverage found its way into our household!

The house itself was an absolute treasure-trove of Victoriana, and as a little boy I was deeply ashamed of its old-fashionedness. We did of course have mostly electric light, but the old gas mantles still worked, and several rooms including my bedroom in the attic had only gaslight. There was lots of gorgeous old Victorian furniture and lovely ornate mantelpieces which today would be worth a fortune. The conservatory, or what we knew as the greenhouse, was full of aspidistras in large pots. These multiplied continually, and the numbers of the containers expanded to fill every windowsill in the house. Grandpa's main household duty was to go round each week with a damp wash-leather, wiping the dust off the broad leathery leaves of these typical Victorian vegetative monstrosities. Even then they were objects of good-natured derision; witness the famous ballad of the Thirties sung by the inimitable Gracie Fields – "The Biggest Aspidistra in the World".

We also had in the greenhouse a large birdcage containing an impressive white Australian cockatoo with a beautiful yellow comb.[3] He answered to the name of Billy and had arrived in the Mountain household many years before, a present from some vague seafaring relative of my Grandma's. He was already very old, but still lively and active, right up until he suddenly fell off his perch, quite without any warning, on my 14th birthday. He was sadly mourned, as he had been a lively presence in the household ever since I could remember. He talked quite a lot, and associated regular happenings in the household with appropriate words. He could clearly hear the sound of the front door, so he always reacted to that, but sometimes he got it wrong. When visitors first arrived at our house, they were often slightly upset to be greeted with a loud raucous voice screaming "Goodbye! Goodbye". His great delicacy was Yorkshire pudding. We always ate this in the traditional Yorkshire way as a separate first course with lovely thick gravy, before the Sunday dinner roast joint. The reason for this custom, widespread in those frugal times, was that it took the edge off everyone's appetite, and the following joint of beef would be more likely to last through the next week for our cold lunches. Mum's Yorkshire pudding was exquisite – I have sometimes tasted it almost as good as hers, but never better. Billy appreciated it fully, and every Sunday dinnertime he would set up a deafening screaming, carrying on non-stop until we fed him a large slice of the delicious stuff!

However, with our trendy new ideas, we tended to sneer at these relics of a past age. Later, when Grandpa became a complete invalid, Mum and Dad undertook a thorough modernization of the house, and all the old furniture and *objets d'art* went on the back of a lorry to the rubbish dump. What a fortune they threw away! All that kind of thing is now highly collectable, but then it was considered the height of bad taste. We had to pay to get rid of it!

Together with the banishment of all Victoriana, the aspidistras also were casualties of the great modernizing purge. The greenhouse was bare of their waving green leaves, and in their place was a large collection of modernistic looking cacti and succulents. It was all undertaken on the assumption that Grandpa would never emerge again from his bedroom, but to the dismay and consternation of all, after about a year of seclusion he felt much better, dressed again and descended to the living quarters. We waited with bated breath to see what his reaction to the great transformation would be, but at first there was none. He surveyed everything with completely expressionless mien, eventually making only one slightly forlorn query in his dour North Country voice – "Wheere's t' aspidistras?"

It is interesting to see how far real definite memories go back. Bertrand Russell boasted he could recall his entire life back to lying helpless in the cradle. I cannot claim to remember much before age five, though I have a clear picture as a very small child of being horribly afraid of going to have my hair cut. I was convinced the scissors were going to cut off my ears. Every subterfuge possible was used to get me to the barbers! I was taken out in the car with the promise of a lovely ride in the country, and then Dad treacherously stopped suddenly outside the barbers, causing me to set up a ferocious wailing which continued during the whole business of clipping, completed as quickly as possible by Mr. Jenkins, the barber, who dreaded my visits! When I was a little older I managed to control my fears to some extent, but even now I can feel some remnants of that sensation:

Further Scrapings

having my hair cut (what there is left of it!) is not the most pleasurable experience for me.

Talking of rides in the country, our family always delighted in exploring the wonderful Yorkshire Dales, just virtually on our doorstep. The contrast between the ugly, smoky industrial towns of the Aire valley, with their "dark, satanic mills" and the lovely Yorkshire countryside, was magical to appreciate. We regularly took the tram into Bingley, and then boarded a single decker bus up to the little village of Morton, finally walking still further up to a delectable spot known as "T' Ouzel Oile", or "The Ouzel Hole", ouzel being an archaic word for the blackbird. This was an idyllic wooded valley penetrating up into Rombolds Moor (or Ilkley Moor). We often stayed a few nights in a little grocers shop in Upper Mill Row owned by Mrs. Taylor, whose son Billy was in my form at Bingley Grammar School. Outside the house a little bridge crossed the stream, and you walked up the valley to marvellous ruined water mill buildings, dating from the very earliest days of the Industrial Revolution when steam was not yet available and water power streaming down from the moors provided the energy for the processing of wool. Still further on was a little hill-top reservoir where I learned to swim. A glorious place for just "messing about"! When Grandma heard we were going up there, she invariably replied "Eee, I 'aven't been up to t' Ouzel Oile since t'Flood!" This was not a Biblical reference, but was her memory of a cataclysmic local inundation in the eighteen seventies.

A couple of miles walk from home took us to Shipley Glen, then on to Baildon Moor, and after that there was a day's hike over Ilkley Moor ("baht 'at!), arriving at the rather posh spa of Ilkley in the idyllic valley of Wharfedale. Beyond that, within reach of biking expeditions, lies Bolton Abbey, then comes the Strid, where the river is compressed into a dangerous torrent between jagged rocks. Barden Towers is a picturesque fortified manor house, featuring on innumerable Yorkshire calendars, and further on there is Burnsall with its beautiful bridge, Kilnsey Crag, and Kettlewell. By then you are in the limestone area of the Craven Fells. A really extensive expedition, starting with a train journey from Shipley to Bell Busk, would take us to Malham, source of the River Aire and perhaps my most favourite spot of all. Malham Cove and Gordale Scar are both extraordinary geological formations always worth a visit. Either by car, by bike in later years, or by bus and on foot, there were endless exciting excursions to be had into this lovely unspoilt countryside. In my childhood memory, the sun always shines on the gorgeous River Wharfe.

From five onwards recollections are much clearer. My first school was Otley Road Primary, just a short distance from home. I recall a kind lady called Miss Webster, one of the teachers, who called at our house every morning to take me across the main road for 9 o'clock prayers and classes. The school had three doorways, one for boys, another for girls and one for the very youngest, which of course included me. Miss Sleighdon, a benign and grey-haired lady was in charge of the class which I joined. I told one enquiring friend that I was not a boy or a girl, but a Mixed Infant, for that was the legend carved in stone above my entrance!

Mum and Dad were good amateur musicians. The World Slump in the late twenties ruined much of the wool business that had supported them comfortably until then. When I was only five, my paternal grandfather, Frederick Mountain, died. I remember him as a kindly, white-bearded presence, looking the very image of a 19th century Victorian patriarch, but he could be very jolly, playing cricket with me in the back yard of his house. He lived in Priestthorpe Road, Bingley, where my Dad had been born, and had started the wool-sorting business that provided his family with a comfortable livelihood. But his demise, followed by the financial disasters of 1929, which spelled the end of many small enterprises in the area, meant that our business, based on its own small warehouse in Bingley centre, crashed disastrously; we were suddenly bankrupt. I remember crying bitterly when men came to take our lovely Standard motorcar away. So it was then, in 1928 that my parents set up as piano and violin teachers respectively, and I began regular piano lessons with Mum followed two years later by violin lessons with Dad.

I am sure it is best to start any child's musical education on the keyboard, being the simplest way to absorb the basics of notation and rhythm. Mum taught beginners with the Mrs. Curwen Method;

a series of books that look dreadfully old-fashioned now, but I really liked them, and they certainly gave her pupils a good grounding, particularly in rhythm. I had to sing rhythmic passages, using ta ta ta ta for crotchets, ta-aa ta-aa for minims, and ta-aa-aa-aa for a complete semibreve. Quavers were ta-fe ta-fe, and semiquavers were ta-fe-ti-fe ta-fe-ti-fe. Further than that we did not go! It might seem to modern eyes unimaginative compared to present trendy way-out books aimed at appealing to youngsters, but I can remember loving it and it certainly stuck in my mind. Anything that strengthens rhythm is good. Shaky rhythmic sense is the commonest failing at all ages, and beautiful rhythm is the first essential of any good performance. Also we were made to do aural exercises, learning to recognize pitch and intervals, and I loved them too, probably because it was found that I had perfect pitch. I feel sure that many people who say they are not able to name notes accurately (in other words do not have an aural memory) do actually have that ability, but haven't developed it early enough. Thanks to my Mum's training, Kath and I always got full marks in the aural tests of the Associated Board Exams, for which we were entered regularly.

Aged seven I left the Primary School and began to attend the Elementary School in Saltaire, about a mile away in the Victorian model village of Saltaire. I used to walk this distance four times a day, coming home for midday dinner, very occasionally spending a penny on the tram journey. No lifts to school in those days!

Saltaire, built during the 19th century by Sir Titus Salt, mill-owner and philanthropist, was a model village, surrounding the immense Salts Mill that was the source of the fortune he made from the alpaca trade. In the twenties and the thirties the mill was still a flourishing concern, and hundreds of workers, mostly women, could be seen, and heard, tramping with wooden clogs from the rows of back-to-back slum dwellings along the cobbled streets to do their arduous shifts. They, and incidentally the whole town, were roused each morning by the sirens, not dissimilar to the air- raid sirens we had during the war that was to come in a few short years. The mill, and the many other mills in Bradford, Shipley, Bingley and Keighley, belched continual plumes of black smoke. Every house had a coal fire, so the whole of the Aire valley was painted black, as was the entire industrial North. The buildings, originally of beautiful peach coloured sandstone were uniformly the same depressing hue. Nowadays, Saltaire, like the surrounding areas, is free from this kind of pollution. The wool trade, for long the staple industry of West Yorkshire has vanished, there are smoke abatement laws, and the stonework has all been cleaned, so the stylish Victorian architecture of the place with its model houses for the work-force, its schools, churches and its Victoria Hall for the general culture of the working people are all beautifully revealed. In 1987, Salts Mill was bought by a local entrepreneur Jonathan Silver and he transformed it into a vibrant place of art and commerce. His school friend at Bradford Grammar was the painter David Hockney, and now the large galleries in the mill are home to a magnificent display of Hockney's works, together with an extensive bookshop, other commercial outlets and attractive eating places – well worth a visit. Sadly Jonathan Silver died quite young in 1997, but the large complex he founded still flourishes. Saltaire is now rated as a World Heritage Site, and attracts a regular stream of tourists.

The school I then attended was called Albert Road Elementary. Memories of this are mixed – lessons I mostly enjoyed, but the general level of inmates was what could only be described as rough. From reading today's papers one could be forgiven for assuming that bullying is an entirely modern phenomenon, but at that school in those days it was already well established. Anyone with such an outlandish name as Mountain was a prime target. I was Everest, Molehill, Ben, Mahomet, torture for a timid seven year old. In addition I was short sighted and had to wear glasses, so was inevitably labelled Four-Eyes. Another burden I had to bear was inadvertently caused by my dear Grandma. I came home one day with a hole in my pants caused by too much activity on the playground slide. She spotted this immediately, saying to my Mum "Dear dear, Dorothy, you can't let Peter go to school like that! I'll see that he doesn't wear his trousers out again" She took the damaged garments and patched them thoroughly with the thickest and stiffest calico; next day I was sent off to school with them on. Inevitably they were noticed straight away, and I was immediately dubbed "Leatherpants". I came home tearfully refusing ever to wear the offending things again, but the taunt stuck for what

Further Scrapings

seemed an eternity. And I played the violin. What could be more worthy of constant teasing, often making life a misery. Coming home from some function where I had to play at the Church Hall, I can recall hiding down side streets to avoid the shame of being seen by other boys carrying a violin case.

However, my self consciousness was eased somewhat, as the Headmaster of Albert Road School, Mr. Mahoney, was a keen amateur violinist, a friend of my father, and a loyal member of the Bingley Orchestral Society of which Dad was the leader, and in which I was soon allowed to enlist at the back of the second fiddles. Gilbert Mahoney (pronounced Marney) was a jovial character although pretty incompetent as a violinist. At one rehearsal when the first violins were berated by the conductor for playing out of tune, he spoke up sharply "Well, it wasn't me. I wasn't playing!" He had a good sense of humour, and used to regale people with stories about his pupils. A class was once asked to write an essay about what they did on Bank Holiday. One effort read - "On Easter Monday, me and my friend went up onto Baildon Moor. We sat in the ditch and played with sheep dirt!" Another week they were asked to write an essay about their Headmaster. This produced the prize contribution – "Mr. Mahoney is a very nice man. He lives in a big house in Shipley, and he has a beautiful set of false teeth!"

The conductor of the orchestra was Walter Dutton. Our family was friendly with the Duttons, and their son, Reg, went to school with me. Although Dad was never a professional orchestral player, he had all of the typical orchestral musician's critical regard for the conductor, and at home after rehearsals he would hold forth at great length about Walter's failures with the baton. To be fair, he could well be excused for this; Dutton was strictly amateur in his musical standards. However, he did have one outstanding quality that earned him his unassailable position at the orchestra's head; this was his striking demeanour and appearance. His complexion was swarthy, his hair wavy, his nose impressively Roman and he had a commanding and direct eye. He also had a most impressive moustache; medium sized and silvery, beautifully parted at the centre and trained outwards. At concerts, he progressed to the podium with a slow and impressive mien. His beat, though by no means completely accurate, was always expansive and wonderfully flowing. His voice was equally fitting to command and impress. He was what one might call a bit of a line- shooter; his erudition when directing the orchestra in musical matters was no match for his impressive delivery, but the audiences loved him! (There are quite a few conductors I have encountered since who have not dissimilar attributes!)

The orchestra gave concerts in the Victoria Hall Saltaire, the small bandstand in Northcliffe Woods behind our house, and in various church halls, but mostly in the Princess Hall, Bingley, which is now the municipal swimming baths. So it was then, during the summer, but in the winter the pool was boarded over and the building served as a concert hall. Our series of concerts, whilst not being of remarkably high standard, were admirable in their own way, with quite eminent visiting soloists, and attracting generally full houses. Schubert's Symphony in B minor, the Unfinished, was a regular item in our repertoire, and whenever I have since played in it, I am transported in memory back to those far away rehearsals and performances under Mr. Dutton's impressive baton!

Chamber music was always part of our home background. Dad was very ambitious for me to succeed on the violin, though lessons with him could be stormy. He expected too much, refused to accept any excuses, and they often ended in tears, with Mum coming in to pour oil on troubled waters. But as soon as I became reasonably proficient, he used to let me play the Bach Two Violin Concerto with him, with Mum providing the piano accompaniment. Even more did I love playing the Vivaldi Two Violin Concerto in D minor, with its gorgeously bold close canon of the D minor triad between the violins which opens the piece, and the heavenly Adagio with its beautiful rocking Siciliano-like rhythm. Many years later I remember taking part in a performance of this great work in the Festival Hall with the Philharmonia Orchestra conducted by Guido Cantelli. He described its slow movement as possibly the most beautiful melody in the whole of Baroque music!

We often had visitors in for musical evenings. Mr. Pullen, a good amateur cellist, was regularly invited. My Mum, when not required as a pianist, was also reasonably competent on the viola for Haydn quartets. But I remember her best as pianist in rousing home performances of the Schumann Piano Quintet. Later, when I was more proficient, I used to play the Mendelssohn D minor Trio with her and Mr. Pullen. She tackled that demanding music amazingly well, considering that she had not had the basic early teaching necessary for real pianistic prowess.

Of all the early musical visitors to our house, the one I remember most was John Atkinson, the local star violinist. He was a talented player, a handsome looking man whose concerts in the area always attracted attention. I remember as a little boy being taken to a violin recital he gave in the Mechanics Institute Hall in Bradford, just after I had begun practicing the violin. My beginner's efforts then were primitive, to say the least, and I still recall the revelation it was to hear that the instrument was capable of such fluency and tonal variety, but above all, of such wonderful sweetness of sound! I longed to be able to play with vibrato – then for me an unattainable goal. But I thought grimly at the time – if he can do it, so can I! That is what every young player has to have – the desire to make a sound. I was so lucky to have this implanted at an early age.

In the inter-war years, John Atkinson spent some time in Pisek, Czechoslovakia, studying with the great teacher Otokar Ševčik. I was fascinated to hear about this, as I was already being force-fed with interminable Ševčik exercises by my father, and this reinforced my desire to play the violin. John Atkinson became an idol, not less so when he decided to capitalize on his fame as a student in far off Moravia, and changed his rather plebeian name to John Morava. I remember Dad was quite scathing about this; he thought it was pretentious, though I thought at the time that he was secretly a bit jealous of John's ability. However, this did enhance his fame in Britain, and he eventually obtained the post of Music Director of the little orchestra at the Spa Pavilion, Llandudno. Years later, when I was in the profession, I heard a BBC recital by John, and decided that he wasn't quite as good a player as I had remembered him, but I was always grateful to him for giving me that initial inspiration.

When my parents decided to turn their musical abilities into real earning capacity, and to set up as professional teachers, they each sought the best teaching for themselves from what was available locally. I have described previously how my father had lessons from the great Arthur Willie Kaye in Huddersfield, himself a pupil of Ševčik, and a major influence on violin playing in Britain. It is a great shame that Huddersfield has so far not been able to commemorate Kaye as one of the city's most remarkable musical sons before his memory fades away completely. Some years ago I tried to set up a violin competition in his memory, but was unable to attract enough financial backing. Maybe others will succeed in some similar venture in the future.

Mum sought help from a remarkable woman in Bradford called Irene Martin. She herself had been a pupil of Tobias Matthay, teacher of Myra Hess, Clifford Curzon, Harriet Cohen, Harold Craxton, and the founder of an influential piano school. Miss Martin certainly helped my mother considerably in becoming a good player and an excellent teacher, and at the same time she became a very close family friend. She was a lovely warm personality, and was especially affectionate towards the children, Kath and me.

Miss Martin was rather stout and quite lame, suffering badly from arthritis. She had a little Austin 7 car, which was her salvation for getting about and generally socializing. She also had a very amiable big white bull terrier called Sam, who accompanied her everywhere. Whenever she got into the car, Sam was invariably asleep in her driver's seat, so she always had to roar out "Hutch up, Sam!" Her only way to exercise the beast was to find a deserted stretch of country road, let him out, and allow him to galumph along in front of the car until he was tired. That generally worked well, though it would obviously be quite impossible today with our traffic density. On one occasion, Miss Martin offered to take Kath and me out for a spin in the country. We were just passing the village of Cullingworth,

Further Scrapings

when she decided to let Sam out for a run on the road down through Harden into Bingley. Everything went fine – we were trundling along about 8 or 10 miles an hour and Sam was galloping in front of us, when suddenly, an identical Austin 7 impatiently overtook us and settled between Sam and our car! Crisis! Sam, glancing back over his shoulder, obviously thought "My God, they're really pushing me!" and stepped up his pace as best he could. Kath and I were standing up on the back seat with our heads through the sunshine roof, screaming "Sam! Sam!" Eventually the poor old dog realized that there must be some mistake, and let the other car overtake him just before we reached the Ireland Bridge over the river Aire into Bingley Main Street!

Chapter 2 - Bradford Musical Life

Like any sizeable city, then as now, Bradford had a body of professional and semi-professional musicians who played in various local concerts, taught both privately and in the schools, and accompanied various choral societies. My parents became part of this community, and much of their home conversation contained discussions about their colleagues' merits or otherwise. John Atkinson/Morava was always talked about, but there were other violinists around, most of who drew my father's often critical attention.

Edward Maude (violinist 1880-1967) though actually more closely associated with Leeds than Bradford, was nevertheless a strong local influence. He was the leader of the Northern Philharmonic Orchestra that flourished from 1908 to 1947. Not only did he occupy the front desk of the orchestra but he was also secretary, organizer and chief factotum of the band throughout its entire life. He contacted and booked all the most distinguished conductors of the day, such as Thomas Beecham, Malcolm Sargent, Adrian Boult, Albert Coates, Hamilton Harty, and many others. In 1932, he appointed the 33 year-old John Barbirolli as Principal Conductor, a post he held for four years, presaging his more notable tenure of office with the Hallé Orchestra after the War.

Unhappily, the orchestra was disbanded in 1947 with much ill-feeling, when Leeds Corporation founded the new Yorkshire Symphony Orchestra in what Maude and his friends considered an underhand way. However, this new venture, although beginning with confidence, did not survive long, and was disbanded in 1952, so Maude must be granted the accolade of having made a much more serious and longer lasting contribution to the area's musical attainments.

I only once played in the Northern Philharmonic Orchestra. It was at Christmas time in 1940, when as a seventeen year-old student, on my first vacation from the Royal Academy of Music in London I was booked to play in Handel's "Messiah" at Huddersfield Town Hall. I vividly remember the performance of "The Trumpet Shall Sound" by the famous Yorkshire player John Paley whom I had met as a young boy and of whom I have written extensively elsewhere. He made this particular number the high spot of the whole oratorio, standing impressively, playing without the music, and slowly moving the instrument from side to side, as if spraying each part of the audience with his golden tones! The conductor, also very impressively, was Sir (then only Dr.) Malcolm Sargent, complete with white carnation buttonhole and appearing just as I remember him many times in later years. Little did I imagine then that within not much over a decade I would be leading orchestras under his baton.

A violinist living in Bradford and working more or less exclusively in the city was Edgar Drake. He was an old-style, dour Yorkshire musician, highly competent in his own way, and able to lead any local ensemble with admirable efficiency, though not with a great deal of inspiration. My parents, together with other local music lovers, had founded an organization called "The Music Circle" which met monthly during the winter months at the Masonic Halls in Manningham Lane. At each meeting, local amateurs and semi professionals contributed to a varied programme, and a more eminent professional would be invited to be the highlight of the evening. On one occasion, Edgar Drake was the visiting artist, and he played the Brahms Violin Sonata in A with my mother as pianist. The performance was, as expected, straightforward, correct, but not such as would lift the auditors inspirationally. I was very amused when, during a few bars rest for the violin, Drake solemnly lowered his instrument, produced a large silk handkerchief, mopped his brow, put it away, then fished out from his waistcoat a large pocket watch which he inspected morosely, put that away and with a resigned expression resumed playing. It looked as if he was hoping that the work would finish in good time before the pubs closed!

Another musician who contributed much to the Music Circle evenings was Frank Mumby, a lecturer in the Music Department of Leeds University. He was an excellent pianist, harpsichordist, organist, and also a well-known musicologist. He was a quiet, bespectacled little man, rather lame, probably from an early attack of polio. My parents knew him well, and appreciated him as an able accompanist, and for the illustrated lectures on music he often gave for the association. I think that it was from Mumby's early example that I began to appreciate that it was good to develop background knowledge of the music and the composers if you wanted to perform successfully. You don't need to be a full-blown musicologist, but if you are aware of more than just the bare notes, you can hope to transmit the atmosphere and meaning of the music more clearly to the audience. Some players are scornful of academic musical studies, which is a pity. As performers, our job is to communicate the beauty of the music to our audience, and it is obvious that the more knowledge we have of every aspect of the music, the better we will be able to do so.

A player of a really good standard was the Bradford cellist Douglas Bentley. Dad admired him greatly, so much so that he began to have cello lessons from him with the object of teaching the instrument himself, both privately and in the Bradford schools. I don't know why he did this; he had left it far too late in life to become proficient on a new string instrument, but he was obsessed with the cello, as he always was with any new venture that caught his attention. My sister, Kath, also studied with Bentley, and the cello eventually became her principal instrument, but Dad was always really an amateur, though with his knowledge of string playing generally he was able to teach most of the string instruments quite well. He never got round to the double-bass, however, which we thought was a blessing! Everyone in the family viewed his efforts as a cello player with a certain amount of exasperation. I remember much later one Christmas day, I think in 1967, when my wife and family were spending the holiday with my parents. They had by then moved out of Shipley and bought a charming isolated house called Eldwick Villa, up on the edge of Ilkley Moor. After the morning distribution of presents, Dad insisted that we play some chamber music, so we proceeded to struggle through the Schumann Piano Quintet, (always a staple item with our family) with him playing the cello. Jeanette, my daughter, now a well-known and highly- talented cellist, was then, aged ten, just a beginner, so she listened intently to our efforts. Afterwards, as it was a gloriously sunny day, we had a bracing walk over the moor with the dogs. Jeanette was walking along with me, and I suddenly heard her quiet little voice saying – "I know it's not a very nice thing to say, but the cello wasn't always in tune!"

Douglas Bentley, however, was someone who played very well, had an impressive style, and was a useful professional in any situation. It is remarkable that the North of England seemed to produce a particular breed of cellists, rather dour and serious, but having good natural tone quality and forming the firm backbone of any orchestral ensemble they led. Examples that spring to mind are Haydn Rogerson, for many years principal cello of the Hallé, whom I heard as soloist in the Delius Concerto for violin and cello with Laurence Turner, conducted by Beecham. But the greatest by far was Raymond Clarke, who led the cellos in the Philharmonia during the time I was a member, which was in the first half of the nineteen fifties. His soaring musical sound is still to be heard in many recordings by Karajan, Klemperer and other great conductors, still reissued from that time. He had a broad Yorkshire accent, a gruff exterior, and you could not imagine a man like that producing the exquisite sounds heard in such moments as the cello solo which begins the slow movement of the Brahms B flat Piano Concerto.

On a different level, there is a probably apocryphal story about a typical North Country cellist being engaged to play in a local church choir's performance of Bach's St "Matthew Passion" with no orchestra, just an organ, and a pianist for the recitatives, backed up by this one cello. The work was progressing rather dismally through its considerable length, and eventually came the words from the Evangelist – "and Judas went out and hanged himself". "Aye", muttered the old chap grimly "I knew summat were bound to 'appen sooner or later"!

The main woodwind player in Bradford was undoubtably the clarinettist Harry Watson. He played free-lance all over the North, and was a very capable soloist. Dad got to know him well, and suggested when I was about twelve that I should learn the clarinet with him. So a B flat instrument was bought, and I began weekly lessons in his little house up in the Bradford suburb of Great Horton. But I'm afraid I didn't take to the instrument too much. I gained a reasonable degree of fluency as I learnt the fingering fairly quickly and could already read music pretty well. However, the main obstacle for me was having perfect pitch, and I felt really uncomfortable with a transposing instrument like the clarinet. I hated the fact that if you read the note C and blew it correctly, the sound that came out was B flat. Also, I couldn't really master the actual blowing process, and the air seemed to escape rather painfully round the back of my nasal passages! So, after about a year of half-hearted attempts, I rebelled, and the clarinet was quietly sold on to someone else.

A few years later, when I was a student at the RAM in London, my girl friend (and later my wife) Muriel was one of the top pianists there, and she took up the clarinet as a second study. As a pianist, she was longing for a chance to play with others in orchestras and chamber ensembles.[4] She was reasonably good at it and became principal clarinet in the Second Orchestra. But my friend Colin Sauer and I used to tease her about her playing, and would always try to make her laugh when she had an important solo to play. When we were married she still had a good pair of clarinets, but she never really forgave me for persuading her to sell them when I wanted to buy a new-fangled tape recorder.

Keith Douglas was a notable figure in my younger days in Bradford. He was born in Bingley, and his father was Chairman and Managing Director of the BDA (Bradford Dyers Association) so he grew up in a rich family. He was educated at Rugby and Exeter College, Oxford. His grandfather on his mother's side (Walter Scott) was the person first responsible for engaging the Hallé Orchestra for the Bradford Subscription Concerts, a tradition that still survives to this day. He studied music in Oxford and developed a taste for conducting. On returning to Yorkshire, he was an enthusiastic supporter of the Hallé, and in return for generous donations to their funds was engaged to conduct several concerts, though from all accounts these were not very good, as his conducting skills were more enthusiastic than expert! However, he did do a lot for music in the area. He started the Bradford Philharmonic Orchestra, a fully professional body that replaced the old Bradford Permanent Orchestra. This operated successfully for a number of years, but Douglas's patience with Bradford finally gave out, when a series of Sunday concerts he had organized at the Theatre Royal in Manningham Lane (now demolished) were cancelled by the Sunday Observance Society. That was in 1932. The next year, Douglas moved to London and became a successful Hon. Secretary of the Royal Philharmonic Society, largely responsible with Sir Thomas Beecham for the foundation that year of the London Philharmonic Orchestra, still one of Britain's finest ensembles.

Dad was always scornful of Keith Douglas's conducting abilities, and his dislike was compounded by the man's capitalist background, which offended Pa's socialist inclinations. He always delighted in telling the following anecdote. In Bradford at that time there was another Keith Douglas, no relation, but he was eminent as the Cathedral and City organist. He was well known to my father who admired him greatly as an exceptionally fine all-round musician, much superior to his conductor namesake. He told my father that on one occasion a lady approached him saying "Excuse me, you will please forgive me asking you Sir: are you Mr. Douglas the organist or Mr. Douglas the musician?"

My sister Kath, when she left school, began teaching at what Mum and Dad had christened The Victoria Grove School of Music. She also taught at Huddersfield Technical College Music Department (later Huddersfield University) as did my mother. Kath became an important figure in musical life in the area, teaching violin, cello and piano. For many years she played cello in the trio at Collinson's Colston Hall in Bradford with Sydney Clarke, violin and Norman Constantine, piano. They were known throughout the North of England and in 1962 took part in the film "Billy Liar". They formed one of the last surviving ensembles of this kind in the country, and it was a great shame when the whole central area around Tyrrel Street was demolished during the sixties in an extremely ill- advised modernization scheme. Bradford thereby lost not only the lovely Victorian Tea-Rooms with beautiful mahogany interior, but also the fine Mechanics' Institute, a Victorian Adult Education institution with an excellent small concert hall. I had played in it at various concerts since earliest days, and in 1955 gave a lunchtime recital there with my wife.[5] In addition, most regretfully, the Swan Arcade disappeared. This was a lovely typically Victorian shopping arcade that gave real character to the city. Some say that by this one act of architectural vandalism, the whole heart of Bradford City was completely ripped out.

Our family School of Music contributed to the musical life of the city by putting on its annual Pupils' Concerts. These began in our front room at Victoria Grove in Shipley, but this quickly proved inadequate, and we moved to the Masonic Rooms in Bradford. With the need to provide a platform for a growing number of pupils, plus the inclusion of items by the Pupils' Orchestra that my mother conducted, we often had to have two or three consecutive evenings of concerts, which were of the greatest value to the young musically talented people of the area.

Although Bradford produced some very fine musicians and there was a worthwhile measure of musical activity, the powers that be in the city did not have a very good record in musical matters during the inter-war years. Bradford possesses an excellent musical venue, the St George's Hall, and before the First World War, my parents heard all the greatest players and singers, together with fine visiting orchestras. Unfortunately, with the rise in popularity of the cinema, the Corporation allowed St George's Hall to become a Gaumont British picture house. Not only was that regrettable, but also it was a very poor, ill-equipped cinema, of the kind known in those days as a "flea-pit!" Thankfully, since the last war it has been restored to its proper status. However, when I was growing up, all Bradford's orchestral concerts and celebrity recitals were in the Eastbrook Hall, a wholly unsuitable Wesleyan Mission Hall. It was there in 1930 aged seven that I was taken to a recital by Fritz Kreisler. I then began to go regularly to the Hallé concerts, in those days nearly always conducted by Sir Thomas Beecham, and had the chance to hear a good selection of the orchestral repertoire at their monthly visits.

Even more recently Bradford had not completely shaken off its reputation for Yorkshire tight-fistedness in money matters related to the Arts. When I was leading the Royal Liverpool Philharmonic Orchestra in the early sixties, we were engaged for a performance of Mendelssohn's "Elijah" with the Bradford Festival Choral Society conducted by Sir David Willcocks. The weather was cold and wintry; it was well before the construction of the trans-Pennine

Further Scrapings

M62 motorway, and the van with the instruments broke down on the way over from Liverpool. It eventually arrived halfway through the afternoon, leaving little more than an hour for rehearsal. Sir David saved the situation marvellously. He topped and tailed all the various numbers in the work; everyone pulled their weight and at the performance there was maximum attention. The result was quite an outstandingly successful concert and we went away, feeling very pleased with ourselves. However the next week, Gerry MacDonald our General Manager said to me "Peter, come and have a look at a letter I've just received from your home town!" It was from the Festival Choral Society and read in effect "Dear Mr. MacDonald – In view of the fact that the Orchestra only did half a rehearsal for the concert last night, would there be any reduction in the fee to be paid?"

Chapter 3 - Bingley Grammar School

From 1934 to 1940, I attended the Grammar School in Bingley, having been awarded a scholarship from Albert Road Elementary. This had been my father's school, and there was still one master, Mr. Carrodus teaching Geography, who had been there in his time.

The school history goes back to 1529, when a number of wealthy Bingley citizens formed a Trust to provide for the education of boys from the town. The Foundation Trust exists to this day, and over the years has been instrumental in promoting various landmark projects. In the early years it is recorded that the provision of shoes for the poorer children was one of its main duties, but over the years it has evolved into an institution arranging funding for buildings and various projects to raise the standard of education. The original site for the school was near Bingley Parish Church, but during the 19th century it was moved about half a mile out towards Crossflatts. When my father attended, it was still a boys-only establishment, but around 1930 a large wing was added for girls. However, in my time it was not by any means co-educational. The door into the girls' school was kept firmly locked and shrouded by a black impenetrable curtain. It was the most heinous of crimes for any boy to venture through this barrier. Playgrounds were similarly strictly segregated. All classes were single sex. The boys were taught exclusively by men, and similarly there was a separate female staff for the girls. Only at the end of my time, about 1939, was there the glimmering of a move towards co-education, with a few sixth form classes being mixed. Full co-ordination did not come until the Fifties.

However, when I was there I do remember that there was some collaboration between the boys' school and the girls' school. In 1937, Macbeth was the Shakespeare play to be studied at School Certificate level, and we put on a week's run of performances in the Princess Hall in Bingley. Obviously, this involved extended rehearsals, mostly in the new hall that was in the girls' wing of the school, and of course with a cast including girls. What a thrill! I was in the very minor part of Ross – a nobleman. Macbeth was played by John White, a sixth form boy, two years older than me. I thought he was terrific and am still convinced that he had real talent, but as far as I know he lived his life in Bradford as a successful businessman. Lady Macbeth was a glamorous sixth form girl, completely unapproachable by me, but I had a violent "pash" on her, thus starting a continuing tendency to fall for older women![6] Aged 14, this was my first major emotional disturbance, and I suffered agonies of unrequited love, being too shy to confide in anyone, least of all to her. A vivid memory is when we were all getting dressed for the first night, and I caught a thrilling glimpse of her bare shoulders: it shook me to the marrow.

I can't even remember her name now!

Probably the most famous old boy of Bingley Grammar is Sir Fred Hoyle, scientist, science fiction writer, and best known to the general public for his concept of Black Holes. He was born in 1915, died in 2001, and attended the school eight years before me. I never met him, which I regret very much, as he comes across in his writings as a fascinating personality.

His autobiography "Where the Wind Blows" is interesting to me, particularly for the first section, giving a vivid account of his boyhood in Bingley. The descriptions of the town fit in very well with my earliest recollections. My father was born there, only three miles from my home in Shipley; Grandma continued living in Priestthorpe Road, Bingley after Grandpa died, and we had many connections in the vicinity, so I was often there, even before I attended the Grammar School. Hoyle's account of his school days takes me back vividly to my own, as quite a number of the teaching staff were the same, and he gives interesting appreciations of their work.

The Headmaster was Alan Smailes whom Hoyle had found very helpful in preparing him for entrance to Cambridge. Personally I found him rather distant and a touch sanctimonious, but he was an authoritative leader, and although the boys tended to mock his rather humourless diatribes, discipline in the school was good, and there was an air of respect, which I am now old-fashioned enough to think is lacking in today's schools. Not that we didn't take plenty of opportunities to poke fun at all the Masters' particular characteristics.

In my year however, we couldn't criticize the Head too much because his son Geoffrey was in my form, and another son Richard was a sixth form prefect, of whom I was much in awe!

The chemistry master, Herbert Haigh, was very well respected. He had been a particular help to Fred Hoyle; in 1932 at the height of the depression, Haigh apparently bought chemistry books out of his own pocket for the benefit of Hoyle and others who were trying to get into Cambridge. He was very lame, from horrific war wounds, but was universally liked and always had absolute attention in class. Not that there were not occasional bold spirits who wouldn't creep into his laboratory before class and substitute the sulphuric acid in the bottles with plain water, playing havoc with Haigh's demonstration of experiments! However, he took these things in good part.

I think, looking back, we had a good bunch of teachers, each with their own idiosyncrasies, which at least served to hold our attention. E. A. Kaye, who taught physics, was another who had been appreciated by Hoyle. He had a mannerism of speech that we tended to mock, but I do remember enjoying his subject. Bernard Long taught English. In contradistinction to his surname, he was not more than five feet high, so was predictably known as Shorty Long. He was also very youthful looking, and could easily be mistaken for a fourth form boy, so much so that he once had his ears boxed by the policeman on point duty outside the school for crossing the road when he shouldn't, in front of all the boys. Mrs. Long, who loved him dearly, was however wont to tell stories against him. One was of when Bernard was doing some work in their front garden, dressed in shorts. A gypsy woman selling clothes pegs put her head over the fence, saying "Is yer mother in, dearie?" He drew himself up to his full height, replying haughtily – "You mean my wife!!"

Eddie Dodd, the senior master under Smailes, was a lively and ferociously intelligent little man who was pretty intolerant of incompetence. He taught Latin and History, and I can date my interest in the latter from his teaching. He also wrote a fascinating history of Bingley, which should have become a classic. I have always regretted not doing Latin with him. In the second year we had to choose between Latin and German, and largely at the behest of my father I opted for German as being more useful for music. So many of the great composers are German, and some, like Schumann and Hindemith, use the language for their expression marking.

The German master was a younger chap called Mr. Mann. I didn't get on too well with him – I was convinced he was a Nazi. He kept telling us that Hitler was to be admired, because like Mussolini he made the trains run on time. All through my days at Bingley there was the shadow of world conflict ahead. Some thought, wisely, that Britain was being weak – others thought that another war like the last should be avoided at all costs. But Mann seemed to us to be blatantly pro-German, which we didn't like.

French was taught by Mr. Forbes, the one master who had great difficulty in keeping order in class. I still don't know what is the exact quality and personality needed to keep the attention of thirty or so rowdy young lads, but Forbes didn't have it. However, he couldn't have been too bad, because my French now is fairly reasonable, whereas what I can remember from Mann's German teaching is more or less limited to being able to rattle off the declensions of the definite article and very little else.

Mr. Fawcett took us in maths. He was a highly-strung individual with probably an excess of thyroid gland. If he suspected any lack of attention, he would begin nervously to throw a piece of chalk up and down from his hand, and then suddenly, with the utmost force, would hurl it accurately at the offending boy with devastating effect. He was generally rather intolerant – very intelligent but not easy to learn from.

"Chucky" Laycock (no idea how the nickname originated) took us in handicrafts, woodwork and metalwork, in what I remember as a remarkably well-equipped workshop. He was a pleasant chap; a first class cricketer and well liked, but he failed completely to rouse my interest in handicrafts. My father used to spend hours messing around in the back stables behind our house enthusiastically cobbling together all sorts of moderately useless articles. I learnt enough at school to appreciate that he was doing everything in the wrong way and was not slow to criticize, but he took pride in his unorthodox methods and had a real flair for what he called "botching" things together, whereas I had none. That kind of ability definitely skipped a generation in my case!

The Arts were probably not the strong point in the staff at Bingley. Mr. Paddon was the art master, and I remember his lessons as being rather boring. He was a mild character, but was interesting to my father as he was a keen amateur violinmaker. Dad used to get him to do repairs for his many violin pupils.

Mr. Thornton came in to the school part time to teach music. He had a hard time with the boys as he, like the French master Forbes, was pretty incapable of keeping order. We were formed into a choir and sang part songs that didn't interest us very much. I remember struggling through "Snow" by Elgar, which I hated at the time and have never heard since. I am sure my dislike was because of our execrable singing. However, Mr. Thornton several times put on very successful performances of "Hiawatha's Wedding Feast" by Coleridge Taylor. It must have made some impact on us because even today I can still remember the words and the music almost entirely. "Hiawatha" used to be staged annually at the Albert Hall in London, in full costume, with a vast orchestra and choir attracting huge audiences and generally conducted by Sir Malcolm Sargent. I remember, much later, a concert with the Liverpool Orchestra playing for the Bradford Choral Union conducted by Sargent. The programme included "Hiawatha's Wedding Feast" and the Choral Symphony by Beethoven. In the interval of the rehearsal, Sargent said to me – "Don't you agree, Mr. Mountain that Coleridge Taylor is a much better orchestrator than Beethoven?" I thought at the time – "You unmusical so-and-so!" but now I can see to some extent what he meant. The composer of Hiawatha may not have the deepest inspiration in his music, but he certainly has facility, and his use of the orchestra is admirable for its clarity. Not for nothing was the young Negro musician hailed in America as a new Mozart. Maybe a new Mendelssohn would be more appropriate, as he appealed enormously to the Edwardian musical public. Apparently he was also an outstanding conductor. Although born and brought up in London, he often visited the USA and in 1910 was described by members of the New York Philharmonic Orchestra as the "Black Mahler". (The composer Gustav Mahler conducted the orchestra up to the time that Toscanini took over.) He was known as a man of great dignity and patience, and his self-expressed aim in life apart from his music was to help establish the worth and position of the black man.

I was sorry not to be able to sing in Hiawatha, but as I played the violin, I was always required to be in the scratch orchestra assembled for this occasion.

Being the only boy in the school who wanted to do music for the School Certificate Exams, I was allowed to study for this with my mother, as Mr. Thornton was only part time at the school, and in any case we didn't think he would be much good at helping me with the syllabus. I entered for these exams in 1939, just before the War broke out. I should have then stayed on for a further two years in the sixth form to do my Higher School Certificate, but during 1940 I was awarded a West Riding Scholarship to the Royal Academy of Music in London, so in September that year, aged 16, I left school and began my musical life proper. The story of how this coincided with the outbreak of the German aerial bombardment of London has been more fully told in my previous book.

I must in fairness to the West Riding of Yorkshire, which has often been accused of a lack of generosity towards the Arts, as noted by me in the previous chapter, now express my gratitude to their Education Department in its generous provision of what were known as County Major Scholarships for youngsters showing particular abilities. Fred Hoyle in his book says much the same, mentioning the support he received through about five years at Cambridge. I was lucky enough to come to the attention of Charles Hooper, then Music Adviser for the West Riding who awarded me the County Major Scholarship for Music which as far as I can remember was £250 per annum. This doesn't sound much today, but then it more or less covered my board and lodgings for the year. When I started at the Academy, my teacher

Rowsby Woof put me in for an Academy scholarship, but this was really only for prestige reasons. It was about £30 a year and barely paid for the Academy tuition fees. In those days it was very much the luck of the draw where you lived that decided the support you got for further education. The West Riding was among the best in the country, whereas Warwickshire, which was where my wife came from, was one of the worst, and her expenses were paid by small value Academy awards and much sacrifice on the part of her parents.

Chapter 4 - Harry Mountain

My father was such a strong influence on me during those early years that he deserves a chapter of this book to himself. It was not that I had an outstandingly affectionate relationship with him, indeed there were often stormy clashes between us, but there was never any doubt that he always tried to do the best for me. I owe him a tremendous debt of gratitude for the very well-meaning upbringing and early violin tuition I received from him.

He was born in 1898 at 22, Priestthorpe Road, Bingley to Frederick Mountain, a skilled wool sorter, and his second wife Naomi Hill. She came originally from Haworth, where her father knew the Brontë sisters and was over forty when she gave birth to Harry. He had an older half brother by his father's first wife; this was Uncle Frank whom we used to visit in Halifax where he was deputy head at Sowerby Bridge Grammar School. Frank Mountain was someone who inspired great respect; he had strong Socialist views and was also a confirmed agnostic. For this reason his career suffered because he would never accept a headship as he could not consider taking morning prayers, then obligatory at all Grammar Schools. His wife, Aunty Rose, was a lovely charming personality – very intelligent also, and so it was natural that they should have two very bright children. Mary was five years older than me, so I always remember her as being rather snooty! She became a scientist and eventually spent most of her time on the staff of the Sports Turf Research Institute on the St. Ives Estate in Bingley, becoming an expert on grass. She never married. David was also a highly brainy person, about a year older than me, but rather frighteningly logical in all his opinions. I remember him saying to me later in life that you should always buy a house to the East of where you worked. The reason being that in the morning when you drove to work, you would have the sun behind you, not dazzling you in the front, and the same would apply when you drove back home in the evening.

From what I could gather, Dad had a sheltered and reasonably happy childhood. He always had an enquiring mind and a keen regard for financial opportunities. He told me that his father was offered a share in the construction and running of one of the two cinemas to be built in Bingley. Dad was enthusiastic that his father should take this up, but his Pa's opinion was that these new-fangled moving pictures were just a passing fad and they wouldn't last. Harry always regretted this lost opportunity; he was sure that the family would have been much better off if this chance had been grasped. Very likely he was right – he had an annoying habit of being right in his sometimes crazy sounding opinions. Later in life, Dad became almost addicted to the cinema. After a hard day of teaching in schools and at home, he would regularly trail across to the Princes Hall Cinema, almost opposite our house in Victoria Grove, and only recently demolished to make way for a block of flats, where he would sit through whatever was on offer, regardless of any real interest in the films shown. He became the forerunner of the present day telly addict!

Dad's financial acumen was specially shown when he attended the local auction sales. To the exasperation of my mother, he would turn up with the most unlikely and useless articles which he was unable to resist buying because they were bargains. He certainly had a flair for spotting things worth the money – even if in some cases they were quite useless to him, but when it came to musical instruments he often hit the jackpot. He came home one day with a decrepit looking violin he had bought for seven and sixpence, or about 37p of today's money. To be fair, allowing for inflation, a realistic figure would be more like £30. However, it was a Lowendall violin from Dresden, an excellent commercially produced copy of a Guarnerius, made about 1900, but it turned out to have outstanding tonal quality. It was obviously a top of the range instrument from this firm, because it has "*Lowendall – Artist's Model*" emblazoned in the back of the scroll. It has a couple of cracks in the woodwork but they have been quite well repaired, Dad got it into pretty good shape and gave it to me; I played it throughout my time as a student at the RAM, and I have it to this day. It still plays marvellously; I would never want to part with it, and it is now worth well over £2000 – not bad for seven and sixpence!

Further Scrapings

Another marvellous bargain he found was when we were on holiday before the War in South West Scotland on the Solway coast. I went with Dad into the nearby town of Castle Douglas. We were wandering around, and happened upon a church building in King Street that had been turned into a junk shop, absolutely full of old discarded *bric-a brac*. This was meat and drink to Dad. In we went, and spent half the morning nosing around this place. He emerged with a cello – dirty and covered with old resin, with no bridge and no strings. I can't remember what he paid for it, but it was something ridiculous. We took it home, back to Yorkshire, and he spent a week cleaning it up, getting a bridge and strings for it and generally putting it in order. To cut a long story short, it turned out to be a very fine English instrument made in the eighteenth century by Peter Wamsley, an exceptionally good specimen. My sister Kath played on it for many years and she eventually passed it on to my cellist daughter Jeanette. It is now her main solo instrument and has a gorgeous sound, equal to many fine old Italian cellos. Instruments by this same maker are now selling in the auction rooms for well over £25,000. Dad just had the nose for this kind of thing.

He started violin studies with John Dunn, famous in the North of England in the early part of the 20th century as a brilliant virtuoso soloist. It was said that Dunn had the walls of his studio plastered with page after page of all the well-known violin *études*, and he would walk around, playing one after another. My grandpa had the means to be able to send his son, who was displaying some aptitude for the violin, to the finest teachers available. But Dad as a young teenager had the instinct to divine that Mr. Dunn, although an outstanding player, was not a very good teacher. He eventually managed to become a pupil of Arthur Willie Kaye, who as I have said, taught in Huddersfield, had been a pupil of Otokar Ševčik and was a major influence on British string playing.

Dad used to tell marvellous stories of his years of teaching with Kaye. Apparently, to get a lesson with the great man you had to be prepared to spend a whole day in Huddersfield in his studio. The pupils sat around a large room, and Kaye would dominate them all. "Right" he would boom "We'll hear you next." And the poor unfortunate chosen would have all his faults mercilessly exposed before the entire class. One boy, who was always castigated by Kaye for not practicing enough, was chosen to play at a session when my Dad was present. Kay asked him sternly if he had practiced properly during the previous week.

"Oh yes, Mr. Kaye."

"Every day?"

"Yes Mr. Kaye, every day."

"Right. Good. Let's hear you then. Get your violin out."

The poor lad reached for his violin case, opened it, and lo and behold it was empty!

"O, I'm so sorry Mr. Kaye, I seem to have left my violin at home."

Kaye reached behind into a cupboard. He produced a violin and held it up on high before the whole class.

"Right, you wretched boy – do you recognize this?" It was of course his instrument accidentally left behind after the previous week's lesson and obviously his case had languished unopened for seven clear days. The ensuing storm of caustic recriminations can well be imagined.

Apparently, Kaye used to prowl round the streets of Huddersfield, listening outside the houses of his pupils who happened to live in the town, to see if they were doing their required scales and exercises. He was the epitome of the completely dedicated teacher, and was terrifyingly severe to all his brood. In spite of this, they all loved him and respected him absolutely, and there is no doubt that he produced several generations of fine players. His work was publicly praised by Sir John Barbirolli, who acknowledged the contribution of Kaye's pupils to the fine string tone of the Hallé Orchestra. His wife, Daisy, was an equally dedicated teacher, and carried on the tradition of her husband's work several years after his death. One very notable early pupil of hers was Rodney Friend, brilliant soloist and leader of the BBC, the LPO and the New York Philharmonic orchestras. John White, the eminent violist and for many years Head of Strings at the RAM in London grew up in Huddersfield and had lessons from Mrs. Kaye. He remembers very well her encouragement of chamber music, and he told me that he considers that she was the finest chamber music coach he has ever encountered.

When Dad set himself up as a violin teacher, it was the principles of Kaye's teaching that were his inspiration and obsession. The ideas were all good, based on the teaching of Ševčik and the publications of Carl Flesch, but they were applied with too much almost religious severity. The correct position of the bowing arm, the left hand, the stance and every aspect of the playing must never fall below the highest level of perfection. Any player who had an awkward looking bow arm or an individual way of fingering was automatically considered beyond the pale.

That leads me to an amusing story told by my son Paul, also a violinist. He was teaching a young girl who was talented but not always careful enough in the details of technique, and so he had to be quite strict in keeping her aware of these basic disciplines. He once was able to get her to view with him a TV programme of a recital by the great violinist Itzhak Perlman. She listened and watched, absolutely entranced. "He's wonderful" she whispered. "He's absolutely terrific!" They listened together for a time in enraptured silence; eventually she turned to Paul saying rather smugly "He'd be even better if he held his bow properly!"

In lessons, Dad used to get quite frustrated if students were not careful enough with these details. When teaching his pupils, he did react considerately when they found things difficult, but with me he often expected too much, and lessons sometimes became a bit too stormy. Mum sometimes had to come in and calm things down, but in spite of this, it was the violin that inspired me, and Dad certainly gave me a very good basic grounding.

I remember when very young playing at local concerts in church halls such pieces as the Intermezzo from *"Cavalleria Rusticana"* by Mascagni – a lovely tune! Later, when I got better at double stops, my favourite was *"Poéme"* by Fibich, and also Kreisler's *"Caprice Viennois"* – a real challenge to play the melody in thirds whilst making a lovely singing sound. Also, for technical speed and fluency I used to slave away at *"L'Abeille"* (The Bee) by Schubert (François Schubert of Dresden, not the great Franz Schubert of Vienna). This is a real finger stretcher, and I was conceited enough to show off with it all over the neighbourhood. *"Praeludium and Allegro"* by Kreisler also would bring the house down – in fact all the Kreisler solos, much in vogue then, were a big part in my development. They are still very valuable to any young player. Being written by one of the greatest ever violinists they are excellent for developing technique, and because Kreisler had an unfailing instinct for attractive melodies and beautiful sound, they encourage the production of both fine tone quality and good musical phrasing.

I must say that in those early days, I was never asked to play anything that was musically tawdry. There are a number of so-called violin concertos written to be played by youngsters, some just in the 1st position, some in the first and third positions, some in what is described as the style of Vivaldi, but they are all pretty tasteless and unmusical, though they are quite good at giving an impression of reasonable competence for the young player. But why bring a child up on second rate music when good quality works and indeed great masterpieces are freely available. What a marvellous piece is the Sonata in A by Handel, and what benefits, both technical and musical, are to be gained from studying and performing it. That sonata was a central item in my younger days, and I remember working for ages on the few bars in the Allegro movement where there is a quasi fugal entry, and you have to sound like two violins playing together! The development of co-ordinations of that kind is the basis of skills on any instrument, and indeed in any physical activity. Sportsmen similarly have to be co-ordinated, and the greatest of them, like good musicians, play their games with artistry as well as technical competence. Many musicians are also keen sportsmen. One supreme example was the violinist Jascha Heifetz, who was a very formidable table tennis player. The story is told that on the last night of a week's trans-Atlantic voyage on board the Queen Mary, he was persuaded to play at a ship's concert. Afterwards, a member of the audience approached him, saying "O Mr. Heifetz, your playing is absolutely superb!" "Thank you very much" replied the maestro. "Yes, it's quite terrific. How on earth you manage to do those backhand slashes is quite beyond me....!"

Although I may have given the impression that my father was exclusively concerned with technical matters in his violin teaching, that criticism is not entirely fair. He did try to instill a feeling for musical phrasing and high quality performance, always emphasizing that the musical integrity shown by a player is more important than mere technical perfection. He had quite a number of prejudices which became more and more exaggerated as he grew older, but they were often based on genuine valid observations or on ideas widespread in his youth. Once Dad had an idea firmly fixed in his mind, it would take a charge of dynamite to alter it! We would tease him about his views on Elgar's music, which he thought bombastic and chauvinistic; nothing could convince him otherwise. However, one must realize that in the years after the First World War, there was a reaction against the country's imperialist past. Elgar was associated in many people's minds mainly with "Land of Hope and Glory" which led to a significant decline in his popularity. When in 1927 his 70th birthday was marked by a special concert of his music, the hall was only half full. The present day widespread appreciation of Elgar is a relatively recent phenomenon, though I think that like all really great men he has never been truly neglected. Early in the 20th century, the great conductor Hans Richter wrote that his life had been largely devoted to the two greatest composers of his age – Wagner and Elgar.

There were several other prejudices I remember battling against. Dad was not particularly fond of Mozart, and thought the violin sonatas to be generally trivial. Here I found him completely wrong, but we must remember that in his early days, Mozart was considered sweet, charming, but without depth; say the musical equivalent of the paintings of Fragonard, with shepherds and shepherdesses revelling in leafy bowers. Also, these works are not primarily violin sonatas, but are really piano sonatas with an *obligato* violin part. Mozart wrote many of them to play himself whilst teaching his aristocratic young lady piano pupils, an occupation which bored him and was only undertaken for the money. But, they are wonderful works for developing the subtleties of musical ensemble. Technically, however, the piano parts are more difficult than the violin, a fact that my wife Muriel never tired of pointing out to me! In fact, it is pretty pointless learning them at all unless you have a first-class pianist, to play them with, which accounts for my lifelong devotion to them. Muriel and I have several times done series of concerts including all these sonatas, even the very youthful examples which are hardly ever played.

When I started as a player, there was a very limited repertoire of Mozart's music performed at concerts. Only one piano concerto, the well-known A Major K.488, was regularly programmed, and today's unquestioning worship of Mozart is of relatively recent origin.

I have already said that Dad had a pretty broad spread of interests He had a good library and read a lot. His subjects apart from music were mainly scientific, not so much fiction, though he had a good knowledge of the plays, and particularly the prefaces of George Bernard Shaw. A favourite book of his was "Science and Music" by Sir James Jeans. Jeans (1877-1946) was not only one of the foremost mathematicians and astronomers of his day, but his second wife whom he married in 1935 was Suzanne Hock, a concert organist. She collaborated with him in writing this popular and readable book, and he also pursued his musical interests by becoming a Governor of the Royal Academy of Music in London. All musicians should read "Science and Music", particularly violinists, if only to obtain a clear understanding of how harmonics work and of the physical basis of string tone quality and how it is produced, which many string players seem to lack.

He also had a great interest in geology, though as in all his subjects he would adopt various hobby horses which he would pursue *ad nauseum*. One of these was the effects of ice age glaciers in the formation of valleys, and I remember him lecturing us at great length on the subject. Several times I became so bored with these diatribes

Further Scrapings

that I used to creep into his bedroom during the morning and find the book he had been reading in bed the previous evening. It would generally have been left open at the page he had reached, so I would quickly read the previous couple of chapters, and I would then be able to counter all his lecturing later that day!

His interests were not by any means exclusively highbrow. He loved detective stories and in later life he devoured these insatiably, bringing back several at a time from the local library. It was through him that I remember developing a taste for the American writer Ellery Queen, and also for the wonderful novels of Dorothy L. Sayers with her elegant and aristocratic detective hero, Lord Peter Wimsey. His taste in entertainment was equally catholic. I used to go with him quite often to the excellent repertory company in Bradford, based in the Princes Theatre close by the Alhambra. The latter still stands and is one of the glories of Bradford. I heard the Carl Rosa touring operatic company there quite often, and the beautifully refurbished Alhambra Theatre still provides excellent and varied entertainment for the city. The Princes Theatre however has been demolished to make way for an ice rink, which is a great shame. The old style repertory companies which many cities used to have were a wonderful training ground for many of our finest actors who started their careers in them, having to act in a different play every week, the evenings taken by performances and days filled by learning and rehearsing next week's play.

Incredible as it may seem, the Bradford Princes Theatre had another theatre called The Palace, built directly underneath it. This was almost entirely underground, and you came off the street at its main entrance to find yourself level with the gallery! It must have been a terrible fire risk, and there is no wonder that it was closed before the War, and was subsequently used as a wool warehouse. However, in my young days it was a flourishing variety theatre, and Dad often used to take me to see the old style variety performers, particularly the comedians from George Robey onwards. A regular Top-of-the-Bill at the Palace was Monsewer Eddie Gray, a master of dead-pan humour, but now almost entirely forgotten. Dad loved him. So did I, and I have certainly inherited this appreciation of good comedians from my father. I think that anyone who performs in any medium can learn from them, as theirs is a craft which depends almost entirely on the skill of timing; which is also what musical performance is all about. It takes real bravery to stand up in cold blood and try to make a dour North-country audience laugh![7]

What other characteristics do I feel I have I inherited from my father? Well, for one thing, I do feel he has passed on to me some absolutely opposite qualities. Having been in close contact with a man of such obsessive ideals, I think I have a tendency consciously to avoid being too one-sided in any definite opinion. I am born under the sign of Libra, which I read somewhere is the sign of the Scales and produces the diplomat and the ditherer; I am true to that, inasmuch as I can generally see the opposite side of any argument. Dad couldn't! His view was always incontrovertibly right. Muriel, my dear wife, was a little similar to him, being Aries, under the sign of the Ram; a pioneer and warrior leader. She was often impatient of my vacillations and thought I was too easily led by every different opinion. However, in my defence, I must say that I have always been quicker than either of them to make decisions, and I resist the temptation to regret past choices. My philosophy has been to take whatever seem reasonable decisions about the future, then to make the best of things. I like changes, but I don't like recriminations about the past and longings for whatever might have been.

I have from him a love of gadgets and new ideas. If computers had been around in those days, Dad would have either damned them utterly, or gone completely overboard for them. Unlike the wise man who recommended all things in moderation, in some ways his motto was - all things in excess! He would consider the wise man a bit of a bore, and in some ways I would agree with him there. I think this was one reason for his strictly teetotal attitude. He probably had a subconscious fear that alcohol might be something he couldn't take in moderation. He did however, in later years, develop the habit of having glasses of sherry in the evening, which mellowed him considerably. He smoked a pipe pretty excessively, which didn't do his health much good. Typically, when he did eventually give that up, it was impossible for anyone, family or visitors, to smoke in the house when he was there.

He had a great liking also for "do it yourself". As I have already said, he used to spend hours in his own little workshop in our back stables, cobbling together all kinds of makeshift carpentry. He acknowledged he was a complete "botcher" in this respect, as everything he produced was unorthodox and essential makeshift, but he was always inordinately proud of the end result. My carpentry and other handicraft efforts from schooldays onwards have always been pretty disastrous, and I always stick to the principle that if you want anything properly done, get a professional in. This was neatly encapsulated by Muriel once, when during some maintenance crisis in our household she memorably remarked "Can you fix this, or do we have to get a man to do it?"

I will always be grateful for what Dad handed down to me. My mother provided what I think is the more reasonable side of my character, but Dad gave me the desire to succeed and the ability to adhere to principles. I may have rebelled against his fixed ideas, but once I eventually made up my mind, whether it agreed with his ideas or not, I think I tended to be reasonably consistent.

Chapter 5 - Music in Schooldays

I have already written quite a bit about music in my early days, but there are some other details that I feel are important to record before we move forward, in order to fulfil one of my main aims, which is to show both the differences and the similarities between musical life then and now.

Without television, without computers, and without the vast amount of present day distraction caused especially to young people by the media and all kinds of consumer products, it was certainly easier in those days to set up home routines to support whatever talents showed up in children. In my case, with supportive parents keen to nurture any musical abilities in their offspring, it was natural and fairly easy to incorporate a daily routine of instrumental practice for my sister Kath and me. I was brought up to feel it was perfectly normal to get up early for a half hour of violin practice before breakfast and school, then do another spell in the evening plus piano practice, homework, and still find time to go out and play with the local lads. I was very lucky inasmuch as Mum and Dad, whilst keen that I should get on, were not too obsessive about music, and right up to the age of sixteen when I left home to study in London, they kept the options open, letting me have a perfectly normal school life with the prospect of either some sort of vocational training or university, or possibly music college. The latter aim was what they really favoured most, but they knew very well that the musical profession was no bed of roses, and a child should not be pushed into it without showing some real ability, and above all a lasting desire to make a life in music. So, it was an agreed conclusion in the family that I would go into music if I got a scholarship to study – otherwise music would be just a valuable recreation.

Both my sister Kath and I were entered regularly for the Associated Board music exams, which I support strongly for providing a graded project of work through the early years and a valuable incentive to keep progressing at a reasonable rate. I also was entered for many of the local competitive Music Festivals in Skipton, Ilkley

Further Scrapings

and Harrogate. People talk a lot of nonsense about the dangers for children of the competitive element. They say that performances should not be judged one against the other, and that everyone should be a winner. However, life is not like that; as everyone knows, there always will be winners and losers, and competition is the life-blood of any enterprise. If you want support from the public, put on a competition – they love it! The thing one must do however is to ensure the competitors realize that to loose is not the end of the world, and if you don't come first, you can always learn from those who are just now a bit better than you. I was looked upon as the local young hopeful, but the more I was exposed to a wider circle of competition, the more I found that there were others around who could snatch victory from me, and that was valuable! I remember Joan Spencer, a violinist from Keighley a little older than I was, who often left me tearful and disappointed at the local festivals. But you have to learn how to lose as well as how to win!

Today we have far more chances for children to be well taught and to reach the highest standards in music. There are special schools which give the best possible tuition for selected gifted youngsters. These are admirable in many ways, but I am not entirely in favour of them. I have seen too many youngsters who feel they are trapped in a sort of hot-house atmosphere and they rebel against it. Children who are highly gifted musically are often equally talented in other ways, and they must be allowed to choose music for themselves. They shouldn't be made to specialize too early. The public has an insatiable appetite for more and more incredible performances by ever younger children, but there is no evidence at all that such a start in life is beneficial later. I can only be immensely grateful to my parents for giving me a balanced upbringing – that is the best start for anybody.

Very often children are guided towards a musical career by over-ambitious parents who love music themselves and want to give their offspring the chances they themselves didn't have. I very seldom recommend children to become professional musicians, which has often led to awkward interviews with parents. To be a keen amateur, which in the true sense of the word means a lover of music, is perhaps the happiest of states for a musical person – making music as and when you wish, and in most cases making a better financial success of life than most musicians do. However, if your personal inclination is really strong, you will become a full time musician whatever anybody says, and in spite of all the setbacks and disappointments, you will have a good life.

If a person has some aptitude and ability for music, there will probably be a definite point in life when the reality of what music is about strikes home, as if entering a new dimension – experiencing a kind of epiphany. It certainly happened for me. I can't recall exactly the date or even year, but I'm pretty sure it was when I was about ten or eleven. I had been doing piano since the age of five and violin since seven, and it was generally accepted that I showed some talent. I quite liked playing melodies, performing, especially playing music with others – it was fun, but no more than that. Then, suddenly one day, I heard Beethoven Egmont Overture. I don't remember where it was, a gramophone record, a wireless broadcast, or even a concert in Bradford. It may well have been at school; we had occasional sessions at Albert Road when a lady used to play classical records to us and talk about the music. I certainly can remember her playing Delius to us and I'm afraid I thought that kind of music was pretty dreary. I was already listening quite objectively to the background music of Hollywood films, and being honest with myself finding it much more exciting, expert and attractive than the classical music I was playing and was expected to like. But the impact of that Beethoven was like an explosion! I'm convinced that at that one hearing I knew it from memory. I certainly have had it firmly in my brain ever since that day. I suddenly realized that music like Beethoven goes beyond words. You can only use meaningless hyperbole – marvellous, wonderful, thrilling, inspiring, and so on. A door is opened into a world of musical experience which lasts for a lifetime. It is like a religious revelation.

Many years later, I remember taking my daughter Alison to a performance of Handel's Messiah. She was about 10 – the concert was in Hanley and I was leading the orchestra. For some reason, I had to take charge of Alison for that day, and she was also with a friend who looked after her during rehearsal and performance. I just

Further Scrapings

hoped she wouldn't find the whole day too boring. However, in the car driving home, she sat silently for a while, then turned to me and said quietly – "I see what you mean now about it being marvellous music....!" I felt that this little girl in her turn had just had her moment of revelation in music – her own personal Epiphany.

Chapter 6 – Random Memories

Is it possible to think oneself back into the years of adolescence and to recall what you actually experienced mentally? I think it is, and I am sure others if they probe a little in their memories will agree. There is a difference between memories which are conventional; have been told and retold until they loose reality and become sort of family legends; and those vivid vignettes which come flashing back from the past with the clarity of photographs and where in the mind you are the same person as today. Smell, sights and feelings are clear, and you feel yourself not a little boy from long ago, but the same person, the same mind, in a different envelope.

I am on the top deck of a West Yorkshire bus travelling through Nab Wood, a suburb of Shipley: a sunny day, but in winter - late January 1936. I am on the way back to school at lunchtime and have just seen the headlines – "The King's Life is Drawing Peacefully to its Close". Strange, but this scene out of the bus window flashes through my mind whenever I think of the death of George V and the ensuing short reign of Edward VIII with the abdication crisis; the only time when England had three different kings within one year. What did it mean to me? Quite a lot, really. It was natural to accept monarchy as a normal fact of life then, without any question, and the morals of that period were deeply discussed. Not that I had had any real contact with royalty or any reason to question its existence. In the papers, photographs of the two little Royal princesses, Elizabeth and Margaret were chocolate-boxy and regularly drew oohs and aahs from adoring ladies. My only previous contact with the House of Windsor was being taken across to Harrogate aged three, when we still had a car, to try for a brief glimpse of King George the Fifth and his Consort, on one of Queen Mary's trips to the antique shops in the town. Apparently it was her way to make a Royal entrance into one of the major establishments, and any particular item that she admired, the management was obliged to present it to her. It was in fact an authorized Royal smash-and-grab raid! I can't remember anything of the grand Rolls Royce swishing past us on North Parade, being far

Further Scrapings

too small to see anything more than large adults' backsides, but I do recall very clearly being taken into Betty's famous Teashop, though this recollection is only due to the fact that I managed there to upset a large cup of hot tea over the whole table, and to my parents great embarrassment, screamed the whole place down!

We were not bombarded with constant media coverage in those days, so the main key events stood out more. Funnily enough they were often associated with a particular bit of local landscape, like that view from the bus.

The year of 1936 with its Royal crisis seems to stick particularly in my mind. Aged twelve to thirteen, in the second year at Grammar School, I was beginning to think a bit more about current events as they might directly affect me. Certainly it was a year when the world turned in a more threatening way towards the possibility and indeed probability of global conflict. The Spanish Civil War, beginning on 18th July and lasting until 1st April 1939 with Franco's victory, was clearly seen by most as a rehearsal by the big bad dictators for something worse. We saw Charlie Chaplin's "The Great Dictator" at the local cinema, and got the message from it loud and clear. Just the previous year, Mussolini had invaded Abyssinia, and on 7th March German troops occupied the Rhineland. All these events produced lasting impact and increased a strong sense of foreboding.

On a lighter note, Kodak had just introduced colour photography for the masses, which interested me greatly as photography was already my hobby.[8] I had a makeshift darkroom at home, and regularly sported tuppence a week for the Amateur Photographer magazine. Also, Monopoly was just invented by Charles B Darrow of Philadelphia and we played it avidly during the pre-war years.

The BBC was already well established. We had a Pye table set and used to listen to the news and occasional concerts, as well as Children's Hour, though by then it was being spurned by me as rather babyish. I had my own cats-whisker crystal set and used to listen on earphones to speedway racing at night in bed when I should have been asleep. The iron bedstead acted as an aerial. The commentator was a relatively young Canadian, Stewart Macpherson, just starting a brilliant career with the BBC which lasted until his death in 1995. One time he was famously voted favourite radio voice of the year, beating Winston Churchill into second place! I used to confuse him with his namesake, the author of "Rudiments of Music", an admirable but dull textbook that my Mum used to bore me with, and was required reading in the first years as a music student at the RAM. The BBC introduced the first public service television broadcasts that year, but this had no impact at all upon us in the far North. Our regular entertainment was the "Pictures" – we would have gone every night if we'd been allowed.

Hollywood meant Laurel and Hardy, cowboy and gangster films, and also Gracie Fields who was a major star in those days. I still think she was an outstanding talent as a popular entertainer. But Hollywood also meant romantic comedies and lovely ladies, coinciding for me with the advent of puberty. My parents, though admirable at organizing our education and well-being, were not much good at helping with the facts of life, especially in my case. I think Kath, coming along over three years later than me was better helped by Mum, but I was left to trying to make sense of the dirty jokes traded around at school, and the growing urges provoked by pretty girls and film stars. I certainly needed some help in this way, and the idea of a girl friend was not to become reality until I left home for the Academy in 1940.

Homosexuality was absolutely not known or talked about in those days, though of course it was around. A vignette that is still vivid for me occurred in November 1936. I am coming home for tea – it is a cold foggy evening, Outside our back gate, the archetypical dirty little man in a raincoat accosts me – I don't know him – I respond to his ingratiating chat rather apprehensively, and suddenly find to my horror that he is putting his hand down my trousers, groping furiously! I wrench myself away, rush into the house and up to my attic room in a terrible state of disgust, and never mention the incident to anyone. The family must have thought I was in a peculiar mood that evening. That was my only overt contact with homosexuality, and it probably had the effect of turning me away from any possible inclination that way. However, it showed me, looking back, how easy and probable it is that children who are routinely sexually abused will, through a sense of guilt, nearly always keep quiet and in effect protect the abuser.

I had many pals of course: boys, with not the slightest sexual connotations that I was aware of. Norman Carpenter was a staunch companion up to 1940, though looking back I'm pretty sure that his constant appearance at our doorstep was because of frustrated yearnings for my beautiful sister! He and I used to have many cycling trips in the Yorkshire Dales and beyond. In the summer of 1940 during what was called the Phony War, we had our last family holiday at the lovely little farmstead of Aikieslack (Fairies Glen), just outside Dalbeattie near the Solway coast. Mum and Dad and Kath travelled there by train, but I invited Norman along and we elected to travel by bike. The distance from Shipley was 160 miles, and we did it in two stages, carrying full camping kit, and staying the night in a field over Shap Fell. We had a wonderful fortnight, cycling, bathing, roaming around the beautiful countryside of Galloway, which is still amazingly overlooked as a holiday destination, and felt roaring fit. The day came to return, and we two lads set off about 6 am on our bikes. The weather that day was awful – a cold drizzle and a penetrating breeze which chilled us to the marrow. We trudged along for mile after mile, laden with tent, primus stove, all the camping gear, and the prospect of stopping in some God-forsaken field, struggling with wet canvas and making pathetic attempts at cooking a meal became ever less attractive. In the end, to cut an excruciating story short, we did it all in one day. The wartime blackout was in force, and over the last fifty miles of pitch dark, my little hooded lights began to give out. We laboured along, in mortal fear of being picked up by the police, too tired to be civil to each other, snapping monosyllables, mostly in grim silence! We arrived home just before midnight, and my Mum opened the door to us in amazement as if we were ghosts! I remember the first thing we did was to eat a large tin of Heinz baked beans and drink a pint of good Yorkshire tea – each!

Looking back again to my earliest days, there are a random selection of events still clear in my mind. The year 1933, when I was 10, marked Hitler's appointment as German Chancellor and the Reichstag fire. Also the film "King Kong" was shown world-wide, creating a furore similar to "Jurassic Park". November the previous year saw the election of Franklin D Roosevelt as President of the USA. His New Deal was seen as rescuing the country from the effects of the Great Slump, and we in this country looked to him as a force for good against the threatening portents in Europe.

By the time I was a little more aware of events, a mixed bag of them appeared in the press and radio. 1937 saw the tragedy of the explosion of the Hindenburg Airship at Lakehurst Naval Air Station, New Jersey – a terrible event which shocked with its large loss of life. On the lighter side was the first of the big scale Walt Disney cartoons, "Snow White and the Seven Dwarfs" which the whole family went to see at the New Victoria super cinema in Bradford. In classical music the year saw the first performance of *"Carmina Burana"* by Carl Orff, but this didn't come into my consciousness until many years later, when its bawdy medieval libretto was still able to shock some audiences.

But now, international news items were showing a crescendo of relentless threats. March 1938 was marked by Hitler's annexation of Austria. After a troubled summer, Prime Minister Neville Chamberlain flew back from meeting the German dictator at Berchtesgarten, waving a fragile piece of paper and announcing – Peace in our Time! What a hope! The country was losing faith with the appeasers; we were waiting for Churchill. That hopeless mission to Hitler was on 30 September: Days later on 10 October the Sudetenland was invaded by German troops – a contemptuous slap in the face for the Allies.

In 1939, worse was to come. Czechoslovakia fell defencelessly to the triumphant German forces on 15th March, and Britain and France did absolutely nothing except to protest. The general mood was one of humiliation, heightened considerably by the news of Franco's triumph in Spain. Most people felt it could not possibly go on like this, and the final invasion of Poland and declaration of war by Chamberlain on 1st September, although a dreaded step, was still greeted with some sense of relief that we were now really going to stand up to the inevitable.

As I have written elsewhere, the day war broke out (famous phrase by the comedian Rob Wilton!) the family was on holiday in our favourite little farmstead Aikieslack near Dalbeattie. Kath and I had succumbed to a form of food poisoning, so the holiday was extended for a week to let us recover. We heard the dramatic news huddled around a little radio in the farm, with a fair degree of apprehension – we definitely expected England to be attacked more or less immediately with bombs, poison gas and whatever else the Nazis could devise. As soon as possible we got on the train back home. As soon as we were home, Dad solemnly organized us and the neighbours to begin digging an air raid shelter in the back garden. This resulted in a rather pathetic and dirty trench about eight feet long and two feet deep. The soil we hit at that stage was intractable heavy clay, and as there seemed little sign of activity from the Germans who were too busy fighting the Poles, we gave it up. In any case, I couldn't do any more digging because I had to go back to school.

The beginning of the war rather neatly marked the end of the first stage of my life. It is true that I did carry on as a schoolboy for the first year, and that time was a sort of interlude between pre-war days and the real years of conflict for the West against Germany. It did see the defeat of France. The wonderful Maginot Line proved completely useless; the Germans simply went round the end of it, through Belgium and then the Dunkirk evacuation was inevitable. Why did nobody foresee this? Surely any half competent French general or politicians constructing this impregnable defence could not fail to think that Hitler might invade the Low Countries, as the easiest way into France. The formation of the Home Guard (Dads' Army!) and much warlike activity followed, but after the first few weeks of the declaration of war and the initial panics, normal life began to run in a strange sort of tandem as it were with the unnatural phenomena of hostilities. It was not until the following autumn that Germany really began to attack Britain with the start of the London

Blitz. Exactly at that time, I left home to begin as a young music student at the Royal Academy of Music in London.

Kath and PM, Victoria Grove 1943

Muriel's first visit to Victoria Grove 1942. Muriel, Mum, Grandpa Wood, Kath.

Wedding 2 August 1945, Haverstock Hill, Hampstead. Truda Brenner, Aunt Mary Dale, Jon Brenner, Aunt Margaret Dale, Beatrix Marr (violinist), Dad, Mum, Margit Brenner (bridesmaid), PM (Marine's uniform) Muriel, Friedl Brenner (best man) Isobel Dale (Muriel's mother, a neighbour, Marcel (Belgian colonel and friend of the Brenners).

Muriel and PM off on honeymoon.

PM by Breta Graham. (Sketched on train journey to Bath Festival with Boyd Neel Orchestra, 1949).

London Harpsichord Ensemble 1952 in the Recital Room of the Royal Festival Hall. Millicent Silver, John Francis, Olive Zorian, Ambrose Gauntlett, Bernard Davis.

Marie Wilson.

Eldwick Villa, on Ilkley Moor. Jeanette, Kath, Muriel, Alison, Dad, Mum, Paul, PM.

Holiday in the former Jugoslavia. Mostar, the Old Bridge. Later destroyed in the Balkan War and subsequently rebuilt. Alison, Paul, Jeanette, Muriel, PM.

Christmas in Partridge Road, Liverpool. Paul, Sammy, Alison, Muriel, Jeanette, PM.

PART II

1940 TO 1955

LONDON

Chapter 7 - Student Days

Although the years 1943 to 1947 were spent in the Royal Marines, mostly based in Plymouth but including much travel, I have included these entire fifteen years under the one sub-heading of London. I began this period as a student in London when I met my life partner, pianist Muriel Dale, and it was in the St Johns Wood and Hampstead areas of London that we were married and set up our home. Gradually we began to think of ourselves more and more as Londoners. Our whole lives lay ahead as London musicians, working with colleagues of similar standard. There was, we thought, no other place worth living in. It was the centre for music, for the theatre (which we loved), and was the only place in the country where the best could be found in every imaginable worthwhile activity. I had moved from what I then thought of as the somewhat benighted North where I was a fairly big fish in a pretty small pond, to the great Metropolis where there was no shame in being a relatively small fish in a great pond of excellent musical fishes and even whales! Today I join with many fellow musicians in the North and elsewhere who sneer at the Londoners for thinking there is no life north of Watford! But in those days, I was definitely one of them!

The start of my life at the Royal Academy of Music in Marylebone Road, just south of the lovely Regents Park, was made all the more remarkable for me because it coincided almost exactly with the beginning of the German Blitz on London. Indeed, the first week or so of the Autumn Term saw me sitting disconsolately in my digs in Vivian Avenue, Hendon as the Academy could not open because there was an unexploded time bomb at the back of the building. I stayed in my room practicing sporadically, walking around the Hendon area, and each night sitting rather fearfully behind black-out curtains listening to the air raid sirens, which were followed inevitably by the drone of aircraft and the relentless thud of the bombs. Hendon lies to the north of most of the activity, but the blaze of fires from incendiary bombs could clearly be seen on the nearby horizon. Only slowly did the search-lights become regularly employed, together with sporadic ack-ack fire, but our defences seemed for a long time to be pretty ineffectual.

From 7th September 1940 to the beginning of 1941, statistics are published claiming that 13,339 Londoners were killed and 17,937 seriously injured. These figures rather put into proportion the relatively meagre efforts of present day terrorists; even the devastation of Baghdad. It does illustrate, however, that attempts like Hitler's to demoralize communities by brutal bombing and fire, if they fall short of absolute obliteration generally do not succeed. Rather the opposite effect is the case. Obviously, we were not told then of the actual dreadful casualty figures, but the devastation was clear to us all. The general morale however was good, and everyone's determination to stand up against possible invasion was truly remarkable. When I returned home for Christmas holidays at the end of that first term, I found people in the Bradford area who had scarcely been touched by the bombing, were almost defeatist in their attitude to the generally conduct of the War, which I remember thinking (as a Londoner already) to be pretty pathetic. The opinion of historians of the time is that by the end of October, Hitler had realized his attempt to break the Londoners' morale had failed, and the Battle of Britain had been won by us. Any attempt at the invasion of the country was then put on the back burner by the Germans.

However, the relentless bombing continued, but was confined to night time, and amazingly quickly life began to resume some of its normal activity.

Only a week or two late, the Academy opened, and student life began in more or less a normal way. The students assembled and lessons, lectures, orchestras, chamber-music and all other corporate activity began.

Someone once wisely said to me that the value a student gets from his academic work in any post-school institution depends largely on the quality of his or her fellow students. In this respect I was tremendously lucky, because I was enrolled in the violin class of Rowsby Woof, the most eminent violin professor then at the RAM. He had at that time a number of really first class students who I have been lucky to have had as colleagues during my entire career.

I apologize for any omissions I make due to faulty memory, but I would like to mention as many as I can of my contemporaries who have helped me then and since by their example and advice. I had a good number of friends at the Academy from whom I think I learnt at least as much as I did from my wise tutors!

The student I met on my very first day at the RAM was violinist Colin Sauer, outstanding player, and about a year younger than me. He was also in Rowsby Woof's class and I think in many ways he was Woof's favourite at the time. Many music lovers will remember him as the leader of the Dartington Quartet, one of Britain's finest chamber ensembles. His cheerful and ebullient personality enabled him occasionally to be ever so slightly cheeky to Woof, and I think Rowsby rather liked that! There were a trio of us who had lessons on a Tuesday morning as I remember; the third apart from Colin and me was Felix Kok, who in contrast to Colin tended to be a bit fearful of our glowering teacher. Woof consequently seemed to take advantage of this and sometimes appeared to bully poor Felix. I was more or less in the middle, with a little bullying and a little praise! Felix, however, was in truth very much appreciated by Rowsby, as well he should have been. He went on to have a long and distinguished career as one of Britain's outstanding violinists, and was for many years leader of the City of Birmingham Orchestra. Woof, who was himself a very fine pianist, gave Felix the rare privilege of partnering him in a sonata recital in the Academy's Dukes Hall in Felix's final year as a student.

A violinist colleague who deserves special mention was Granville Jones, also a pupil of Woof. He was an exceptionally fine player, and I think, looking back, that he had an individual quality in his playing that put him a little apart from the rest of us. He had his full share of Celtic character, with not a little moodiness, and was certainly mature artistically beyond his years. After the war, he was quick to find several prestigious appointments, leading the Philomusica of

Further Scrapings

London with Thurston Dart, and also leading the LSO from 1955 to 1956. His chamber music playing was exceptional, and I was very happy to do a series of quartet concerts with him as leader in 1966. It was a great tragedy that he was killed in a traffic accident shortly after this. He was driving home after playing a lunch-time string trio concert with Kenneth Essex, viola and Amaryllis Fleming, cello. Amaryllis told me that he drove off in a great state, because he felt that he had not played his best. Knowing his temperament, I can well imagine this might cause some lack of concentration. He collided with another vehicle coming out of a side street, was thrown out into the road and banged his head on a pillar box, dying instantly. If only he had worn a safety belt (not common then) he would have lived. He should have been able to contribute much more to the country's musical life.

Ernest Scott was already a second year student when I arrived. As a fellow Yorkshireman from Wakefield, he has been a lifelong friend and valued colleague ever since those early days. He was leading the second violins in the Boyd Neel Orchestra when first I joined, and we often sat together in the Philharmonia. When I left in 1955 for Liverpool our paths parted, but now, both retired in the North, we often meet for sessions of duet playing and reminiscing about the old days!

Pat Halling was a real character, with abundant talent, and a technique which put most of us to shame. He was liable to get into trouble with the powers that be – I remember him turning up to play some solo Bach at an Academy concert dressed in a scruffy sports jacket and an open necked shirt. He was made to borrow something a bit more formal, and appeared on the platform in a dark jacket far too small for him with the sleeves up to his elbows. Nothing daunted, he dashed off the Bach E major Praeludium with the utmost aplomb, bringing the house down, and even evoking a reluctant smile from the austere face of the Principal, Sir Stanley Marchant, sitting in the front row of the audience.

Pat went on to make a career mostly in light music. Nothing to be ashamed of in that. London has and does produce the finest session musicians of any capital city world-wide, and players like Pat willingly accept the anonymity of the recording studios for the satisfaction of producing immaculate backgrounds to our popular entertainments and advertisements. Another satisfaction is that the money is pretty good!

Someone else who made himself a similar career was William Armon. We knew him then as Bill Tilley. He was a lovely chap from the depths of London's East End, and he also joined Woof's class the same year that I did. Changing his name to something more sophisticated didn't change him for all his many friends. He was always warm, friendly, good for a laugh, and above all a terrific fiddle player. A piece that many of us had a go at in those student days was the Saint Saens *"Introduction and Rondo Capriccioso"*. Bill really made this lovely music his own, especially the solo sequence of chords towards the end and the final semiquaver Presto which he played with real bravura! Sadly, Bill died some years ago, but anyone who would like to see an image of that nice man, should watch a replay of the Morecambe and Wise show on the BBC which features Andre Previn trying to accompany Eric Morecambe as soloist in the Greig Piano Concerto. This includes the wonderful episode when Previn despairingly shrieks at Morecambe – "You're playing all the wrong notes!!" To which Eric forcibly retorts, grabbing Previn's jacket lapels – "Listen Sunshine; I am playing all the right notes: not necessarily in the right order!!" So when you watch this replay, look out for the chap who is sitting at the back of the small string section, absolutely laughing his head off! That's Bill.

Ivor McMahon was another Woof pupil at that time who was with me later in the Philharmonia. However, Ivor's main activity was later much more directed towards chamber music. He married the fine violinist Nona Liddell and they both played principal roles in the English Chamber Orchestra. Ivor's main legacy is probably his role as second violin to Manny Hurwitz in the wonderful Melos Ensemble.

Manny Hurwitz himself, a player who is one of my greatest inspirations, had already left the RAM as a student when I arrived, and also he had not studied with Woof. His teacher at the Academy was Sydney Robjohns, perhaps not such a charismatic figure as Rowsby, but Manny spoke and wrote very warmly about him, which is recommendation enough for me. Jurgen Lauland, who was still there during my time, also studied with Robjohns. He was second violin in Manny's original string quartet, and I remember looking up to him as an impressive figure.

Woof occasionally also taught viola players. One who I remember well was Stanley Popperwell, who made a good career in Cardiff University as a member of the chamber ensemble there, and also had a reputation as a musicologist. But the violist I remember best in Woof's class was Rosemary Green. She had the loveliest sound, and a really instinctive musical approach to everything she played. I did many memorable concerts with her when we were both members of the Boyd Neel Orchestra. Boyd allowed me to form the Boyd Neel Chamber Ensemble, which included Ernest Scott, Pat Halling and of course Rosemary. The cellist was the eccentric, irrepressible, Hilary Robinson, and the bass was the equally lively Francis Baines. One summer concert was an open air event at Ken Wood on Hampstead Heath. The high spot of the programme was the Mozart Oboe Quartet with, of all people, the great Leon Goosens as the oboist. We as young players were suitably overwhelmed by the chance of collaboration with someone who was already a legend, but Leon was absolutely charming and put us all at ease. Incredibly enough, just as we were about to start the quartet, he dropped his oboe, grabbed for it, and inadvertently kicked it into the floral decorations surrounding the platform. A member of the audience rushed forward, grabbed the instrument and handed it back to him. Leon was imperturbable – just did a quick – peep-peep – and off we went!

Rosemary Green was the only other person during my time who received the accolade of doing a final year's recital accompanied by Rowsby Woof. I remember attending it and being most impressed by the Viola Sonata of Arnold Bax. It still amazes me that the British in those days, and to some extent even today, allow themselves to be considered by the continentals as a second rate nation musically. Our heritage is not just Purcell, Elgar and Benjamin Britten. People like Arnold Bax are examples of a vast number of sensitive and worthwhile composers that we are only just beginning to value properly. Many of them, like Bax, have their roots in the Celtic fringe of these islands. I think also in this respect of E J Moeran, a composer whom I met, and whose music I have often played, conducted and enjoyed.

When it came to my turn to do a third year recital, I was already firmly established in a duo partnership with Muriel Dale. We were yet to be launched under her stage name of Angela Dale, but we were already rehearsing and playing violin and piano sonatas together regularly. The main item we did in that concert was the Beethoven Sonata in C minor Opus 30 No. 2, which has always been one of our favourites. Muriel also played as a solo item *"L'isle joyeuse"* by Debussy, and I did the Saint Saens *"Rondo Capriccioso"*. It was felt that if the pianist was playing solos and duo sonatas, it was not appropriate to be in the same programme a mere accompanist as well, so I obtained another student, Betty Eggleton, to play the piano part in this. The Academy at that time seemed particularly well endowed with beautiful lady pianists, and if I had not already been firmly committed to Muriel, I could easily have been seduced by Betty! She was a lovely, vivacious girl, who played the flute equally well as the piano, and the one thing that kept our relationship absolutely platonic was that Betty was firmly taken as a girl friend by my friend, Bill Armon!

In my early innocence, I had no notion how much or how many actual sexual relationships were going on in those days, but boy and girl friendships and flirtations with a certain amount of what might be described as canoodling were much in evidence. My first two terms were taken up with a pretty cellist called Mollie Eden who commanded my free time most weekends. Mollie was one of those girls whose coquettish behaviour and attractive appearance made her feel entitled to the services of a male escort, without which she would not feel properly dressed. I, as an inexperienced newcomer, was taken on in this way, whilst being firmly assured that there was another official boy-friend in the background who was a superior Air Force officer, and I was to act just as a *pro tem* substitute. She was obviously much better off than I was, having digs close to the Academy in Devonshire Place, near the prestigious London Cello School run by her teacher Herbert Walenn who was also the main cello professor at the Academy. I was allowed to meet her outside the house at 2 o'clock on Sunday afternoons. We would walk very properly by the lake in Regents Park, maybe feeding the ducks, then a genteel tea and cakes in the Kardomah restaurant, Baker Street, where she would surreptitiously slip over her share of the bill, so that I could do the real male thing and pay it. Finally, a visit to the Classic Cinema, also in Baker Street, for possibly a romantic Charles Boyer or Bette Davis film. If I was lucky, there might be some brief holding of hands, then back to Devonshire Place for a quick peck on the cheek, and that was that! When at the beginning of 1941 I moved into the student digs in St John's Wood, there was much ribald teasing of me, especially by the girls there, as Mollie's little toy-boy. So poor Mollie didn't last too long, in the face of real competition from Muriel. As she was over four years older than me, Muriel herself got teased for baby snatching, but I didn't care. This was the real thing!

The London Cello School founded by Herbert Walenn was a very strong influence at the Academy. As far as I could see, Walenn ran it as a sort of cello annexe to the RAM. He had produced an impressive list of past pupils, starting with John Barbirolli, Douglas Cameron, the great Canadian woman player Zara Nelsova and many others. In my time he had as students Peter Halling (brother of Pat), Lawrence (known as Frankie) Leonard, with whom I did some chamber music but eventually became known as a conductor, and the impressive figure of Joy Hall. Joy was a couple of years ahead of me – a strikingly attractive figure, playing with great style, but to me she was completely unapproachable! Sylvia Bor, another of Walenn's cellists, came from an impressive family of musicians. I played in a quartet later with her and her brother Edward (Teddy) Bor. Their cousin, Sam Bor, I knew much later as leader of the Scottish Symphony Orchestra, and another sister was pianist Hilda Bor who was very well known as a teacher and at one time gave piano lessons to the young Princesses, Elizabeth and Margaret.

My Muriel was a prominent member of the piano fraternity, and I was inordinately proud when she won the Macfarren Gold Medal as the outstanding pianist of her year. In my previous book I have written quite a lot about Ronald Smith, who was by far the most impressive pianist the Academy produced in those wartime years, but as I have just now indicated there was quite a clutch of attractive girl keyboard players that I would like to recall as best I can.

Jeanette Pearson was a close friend of Muriel's. The two were not dissimilar in appearance and often were confused (though not by me!). Joyce was also a good viola player and for some years was a member of the BBC Symphony. Eventually she married Gerald MacDonald, who became General Manager of the Royal Liverpool Philharmonic during the time I was leader, so we were family friends for many years.

Margie Ley was another great friend. She was an attractive, strong personality who played in an almost masculine manner. I remember playing the Brahms C minor Piano Trio with her at several concerts. She never really followed up a professional career which she could well have done, but had a satisfying family life. We always kept in contact with her. Her performances had great character, and she kept in practice throughout her life. I was saddened recently to hear of her death, but greatly touched to receive from her husband a lovely photograph of Margie in characteristic pose at the grand piano. Obviously it was taken some years ago, but it was wonderful to discover that visible on the table by her side was a framed copy of a long-ago publicity photo of Muriel and myself!

Priscilla Stoner was a sensitive, gentle person who played the piano with obvious musicianship and care. Everyone liked and respected her as a player and as a friend. She married John Kennedy who led the RPO cello section for Beecham, and who I knew when he occasionally led the cellos in the Boyd Neel. We were sad when the marriage foundered and John left for his home in Australia, dying, some say, of alcoholism. This was after the birth of their only child, the impressive violinist Nigel Kennedy. Nigel's assumed bad-boy personality is just about as far different from his mother's character as one can imagine! However, having at one stage known him quite well, I will always respect Nigel's fantastic ability, and also the basic sincerity of his musical ideas.

Ivy Dixon was an outstanding talent at the time. In addition to being a first rate pianist, her instrumental abilities were amazingly widely spread. Apparently, the year before I went to the RAM, she had done a concert there in which she played three concertos, one for piano, one for violin, and one for cello, as she was studying all three instruments at that time! This kind of ability made her ideal for the job she later had for a number of years as the second Director of the National Youth Orchestra Great Britain, taking over when its redoubtable founder Dame Ruth Railton retired. Ivy continued Ruth's indomitable insistence on absolute discipline and devotion from all members and staff, and certainly produced some great results. She invited me to coach the violins for the year 1967-68, and as I have written elsewhere, the string playing in the Bartok Concerto for Orchestra which was given in Aberdeen led to my being recommended for the post of Concertmaster of the BBC Training Orchestra. However, as soon as I accepted this, Ivy automatically sacked me from the NYO. She considered I was treacherously joining a rival establishment! Nothing could be further from the truth. The NYO was a part time appointment, working with young people up to the age of 18 for a few weeks a year. The Training Orchestra was a full-time job, playing with and directing post graduate players in their early twenties. I could easily have combined both, but nothing would convince Ivy that I would not inevitably be involved in some sort of industrial espionage!

Peggy Hubicki was a pianist who was also a most sensitive and prolific composer. She was already married to the violinist Bohdan Hubicki, a Hungarian who was one of Woof's very greatest students. Horrifyingly, in the early days of the Blitz, their house suffered a direct hit. Bohdan flung himself over Peggy to protect her from falling masonry and was fatally injured; she survived but was badly hurt. I never knew Bohdan, but Rowsby was deeply shocked by this, and often quoted him as an example to the rest of us. Peggy had a lot to do with the foundation and general running of the Yehudi Menuhin School at Stoke D'Abernon for gifted young musicians. She always kept in touch with Muriel and me, only dying very recently. She was a sweet and warm friend.

Other pianists included Joyce Hedges, Jean Mackie, Joyce Riddell; the list goes on and on. All these were really excellent, but I hope and think that I have mentioned the ones who were closest in those days to Muriel and me.

In January 1941, the start of my second term at the Academy, I moved from Hendon where I had been staying with family friends, into a large house in Marlborough Place, St Johns Wood which provided lodgings for students and others, mostly connected with the Academy. I have written quite a lot about this in my previous book, but this period was such an important part of my story that I feel I must return to it again.

Chapter 8 – Marlborough Place

The move to these student digs in St Johns Wood really signaled the beginning of my student life proper. It was the catalyst which gave me more of the confidence I needed at that time, both in music and socially, to grow up a bit and learn to integrate with colleagues.

Marlborough Place was to be my home for two and a half years. There I met many friends, had good times, disappointments, successes, went through all the moods and worries of adolescence, but instead of moping alone with all these troubles, I had pals who helped me out of the worst worries and I could compare my tribulations with theirs. Shared troubles are the easiest to cope with. The background of nightly air-raids was in some way helpful – it put our petty worries into perspective, which I think it did for all Londoners at the time. Looking back, I can remember more than anything that in this household of lively young people, in the middle of world shattering events and the realities of war, we had lots of innocent fun!

The most important thing for me by far, was that it was where I met my wife to be; Muriel Dale. She arrived at the same time I did. Being older than me, she had been at the Academy the year before the war, but in September 1939 her parents had insisted that she should not return to the supposed greater dangers of London, and must stay in the safety of Coventry! A year of seclusion there had led on the previous 14 November to Muriel being the last person to play on the organ of Coventry Cathedral just a couple of hours before it was destroyed by the German Luftwaffe. Shortly after this her father died of cancer. The family house was bomb damaged. When the Academy wrote to say Muriel's scholarship would lapse if she were absent any longer, her mother agreed she might just as well return to her studies.

Margaret MacDonald was her friend at Marlborough Place – also a piano student at the RAM – a very open-hearted, rather boisterous, forthright girl from Torrington in Devon, who remained our friend for many years to come. It was heartbreaking to hear that after returning to Devon and living a happy married life, she was stricken with multiple sclerosis and died relatively young after a long and debilitating illness. No-one could be more positive, forthright and happy than Margaret – it is sad how this kind of thing can strike down the most undeserving person.

In those days, life for all of us, in spite of wartime worries, was happy and we looked forward positively to the future. I have mentioned earlier some of the other boarders, like the pianist Tamara Coates, daughter of the famous conductor Albert Coates. Also the opera singers Rosina Buckman and her husband Maurice D'Oisley, both of whom taught at the Academy.

There was one young chap whom I rather wish I had been able to keep in touch with. His name was Neil Gunn. I seem to remember he came from Edinburgh, and he was not a student, though he was about our age. I think his family was quite well-off, and he had been apprenticed by his father to some financial institution in the city. Neil joined in with our circle of music students very easily, being a gregarious type, and we liked his company. He was a keen amateur pianist, though self-criticism of his abilities was something he could not be accused of! Every day after returning from his offices, he would plunge into a flamboyant attack on the Greig Piano Concerto, completely oblivious of the fact that the house contained several pianists who could play his head off, and who suffered aural agonies from his dodgy rhythms and handfuls of wrong notes. It was a bit like having Eric Morecambe in residence! We were all terribly rude about his playing, but all our howls of protest were like water off a duck's back! He thought he was marvellous. However he was a good party animal and fun to have around, and I suppose he made us budding musicians feel we were actually quite good!

One other inmate I must mention. When I had been in the house for a few weeks, a lady arrived with her son, a new violin student. He had been enrolled in the Academy with a very good scholarship, and now she was establishing him as a boarder at what had been recommended

Further Scrapings

by the Academy as suitable lodgings. Somehow or other she singled me out as a person who would help him to settle down in the Great Metropolis. "Would you take care of John and watch out for him?" she said. "He's never been away from home before – I'm sure you will be kind to him and help him all you can."

So, I was saddled with this lad, John Kirkland, about my age, quiet, shy, who followed me around every day. The girls were very amused at this, calling him Peter's little shadow! I had him on the bus to the Academy, at lunch in the canteen and home again in the evening. John didn't say much, but he was a striking looking person. Wavy brown hair, big dark eyes, pale romantic looking face, lovely artistic hands; just like a Byronic hero from a 19th century novel. He had been brought up in a mining village in Derbyshire, his father had been killed in a pit disaster, and he had displayed such extraordinary talent on the violin that the whole community had clubbed together to send him to London to study. This beautiful handsome appearance, which should have sent the girls mad, was partnered with a speaking voice of the most lugubrious Midland accent imaginable, seeming to emanate straight from the coal-face! There was no doubt, however, that John was an outstanding talent. He had come to the notice of Arthur Catteral, one of Britain's most distinguished violinists who taught a few pupils at the RAM, and who had snapped John up as a real find. John could play the most demanding technical repertoire with incredible ease and beautiful sound, which was the envy of us all. Unfortunately, as often happens with people so blessed, he found playing very easy, and the idea of practicing for hours on end seemed to him pretty pointless. Whilst we worked, he much preferred to go to the pictures, and the Swiss Cottage Odeon cinema was where he spent too many of his free afternoons.

He was my silent and rather depressing companion for a few weeks, and I was beginning to feel slightly browned-off with this continual association. One evening, a whole crowd of us were invited out to a birthday party in a nearby large flat. We took John along with us; he sat quietly in a deep armchair, and as far as I could see just had half a pint of cider to drink. Alcohol must have been completely unknown to him, for someone suddenly said "Hey, John's passed out!" We had to more or less carry him home, up the stairs, and into his room which was like a tip! We undressed him and put him to bed, and he slept until midday next day. However, this experience did him the world of good. He suddenly became the life and soul of the party, always ready with any hare-brained scheme, flirting with the girls, never at a loss for words, and eventually he was the one who looked after me, rather than the reverse!

It was sad that John never really developed his great talent, because he could certainly have become an outstanding player. In later life he earned a comfortable living in the session world, but was always content to play a subordinate role in anything he did. But whenever I met him it was a great pleasure because he was always a warm hearted and loyal friend.

Another player who also did light music exclusively later on was the violinist Joe Bloch, who, like Manny Hurwitz, was a pupil of Sydney Robjohns. As could be deduced from his name, he was Jewish, and no-one could have looked more Jewish. He was fairly small, quite rotund, dark-featured, hook nosed, and with that appearance it was all the more of a surprise to find that Joe spoke with the broadest of Glaswegian accents. He was another player with a terrific technique which put me quite to shame. I remember him playing the Paganini D major Concerto with the First Orchestra conducted by Sir Henry Wood. I was already quite friendly with Joe, and I was always most grateful to him for his advice. When I said I would never be able to tackle Paganini, he would have none of it, saying that I only needed some determined work, and insisting that I began work on the Caprices, which gave me the impetus I needed just at that time. The best teachers are often your nearest companions.

Arthur Catterall had another good student at that time, who as it happened was also Jewish and also came from Glasgow. This was Ella Bowe, who was already an impressive figure at the Academy when I arrived. She seemed to me then to be similar as a person to the great young player Ida Handel, though obviously not quite in her class. I think she rather had her nose put out of joint when John Kirkland arrived as a fellow student showing such natural talent, but she need not have worried, because as I have said, John didn't work enough, whereas Ella was very industrious. After her student days, Ella went back to Glasgow where her father, Bill Bowe, was a respected violin teacher and a dealer. I knew them both when I was in Scotland much later, and I was always rather surprised that Ella had been content to limit her career to membership of the violin section in the BBC Scottish Orchestra.

Whenever one speaks of string players, one also thinks often of their instruments. One's violin becomes an integral part of one's life – not a day or practically an hour goes by without carrying it around, getting it out for practice, quartet playing, orchestral rehearsals, concerts, tuning it, checking it's OK. It's like your baby! My little wooden infant for the first couple of years at the RAM was the trusty Lowendall that Dad had bought for seven and sixpence, and it served me very well. We young fiddlers often had sessions in the Duke's Hall in the Academy, trying out our instruments against each other, and the Lowendall stood out very well against much more valuable competition. However, in my final year, with the important third year recital coming up, Dad finally let me have his lovely Petrus Ruggerius, made in the North Italian town of Brescia in 1685, a superb specimen from the school of Nicola Amati of Cremona. It had a lovely silvery sound, and as I have written elsewhere, one of the great tragedies of my career was when it was stolen from me in Vienna when I was on tour with the Philharmonia in 1953.

Francesca Woodhouse, a talented pupil of Woof, rather put us all in the shade because she possessed of all things a genuine Stradivarius, the greatest name of all in the annals of violin making. Antonius Stradivarius (to give him his Latinized name, which was often used in his lifetime) learnt his craft from the great Nicola Amati in Cremona, as did my Ruggerius, and he went on to live for over ninety years, making instruments to the end, earning the greatest reputation of any maker before or since. However, Francesca's instrument was not really in the very highest rank. When Stradivarius died in 1737, he left several unfinished violins and fragments of instruments, and these were subsequently put together by his two sons who worked as apprentices in his workshop. So Francesca's violin was certified as being by Ombono Stradivarius. It was still a superb specimen and a wonderful thing to appreciate and to play on.

There were three other girls in Woof's class at that time who were each remarkable in their own way.

Nellie Ansermiére was a highly temperamental Swiss-French lady with very definite opinions on every subject and who brooked no opposition from anyone, least of all Rowsby. I am pretty sure he was actually rather frightened of her, which was quite amazing, considering his reputation as a fearsome, tyrannical figure! I remember there was a prize at the RAM to be competed for which had as the test piece the Sarabande, Double and Gigue from the Bach Partita in B minor for solo violin. Three people were entered for this – Nellie, Colin Sauer and me. I was having a lesson with Woof one day, and we were working on the Double, which is written in continuous triplet quavers. These are bowed in varied slurs and separate notes. Rowsby pointed this out to me, saying – "Nellie doesn't like these slurs – she thinks they are editorial and it should be separate bows throughout, but between you and me, boy, she's a bit of a fanatic! You do the slurs – they're quite nice!" So I did.

Nellie was convinced that she would win – she was contemptuous of what she thought was the meagre opposition, and in any case she was a mature student, much older than us. I worked hard at the movements, but Colin, rather high-handedly only tackled them a couple of days before the event, determined to take Nellie down a peg or two. The day dawned; we all played in front of the adjudicator, who was the then well-known virtuoso Eda Kersey. I was conscientious; Colin having nothing to lose just went for it and played his heart out. The results – Colin won, I came second, and Nellie was last! Oh dear, what tantrums and tears poor Rowsby had to put up with – Colin didn't deserve to win, I was a nonentity, it wasn't fair!!! Being a good loser was not part of Nellie's equipment.

Speaking personally, what I valued most from that event was the wise and perceptive judgment given by Eda Kersey, who was critical but encouraging in the best possible way. She was a great player, almost completely self taught. Muriel did a joint recital with her some years later, and there is still available in the catalogues a recording of her playing the Bax Violin Concerto conducted by Boult.

The player who stood out to me in my first year was undoubtedly a girl already in her final year, Marjorie Lavers. She was a petite blonde, with what I thought to be a rather superior air – but then, I thought, she's got something to be superior about. I hardly dared address her, and when I heard her playing some solo Bach (I think it was the Chaconne) I was absolutely bowled over by the perfection of it. I had grown to think of the Bach Sonatas and Partitas with their big scratchy chords as a titanic struggle of the violin against Bach (with Bach generally losing!) and here was someone who made it all sound calm, pure and effortless. Her presence on the platform was quiet, confident and completely without affectation. Maybe she could have done with a bit more histrionics in her performance, but I was certainly impressed. I was surprised that she did not make more of her career. For several years she was second violin in the quartet led by Olive Zorian, an ensemble much favoured by Benjamin Britten. Olive was certainly a more exciting player, but Marjorie provided the firmness and control needed in the centre of the web of sound that constitutes a string quartet. The other members of this important ensemble were Winifred Copperwheat, viola and Norino Semino, cello.

Doreen Cordell was the third girl I remember. She was a strong player with much verve in her performance, but I chiefly remember her for her older sister, Joyce, a most sensitive cellist whom we knew much later in Bristol when I was there with the BBC Training Orchestra. Joyce had married and moved down to the West Country, living in a wonderful cottage in the depths of a forest near Bath. Muriel and I met her, and did many very successful Piano Trio concerts with her. More importantly, she took our daughter Jeanette under her wing, and became the greatest influence on her as a cello teacher before she went on to Dartington. Joyce had a superb, quite unique Guarnerius cello which it was a great pleasure to play with. It was not a concerto instrument, but for chamber music it was superb.

Together with these was a violist, Marjorie (Bunty) Lempfert. I was always rather surprised that Woof took on several viola students, as there were good viola teachers already at the Academy, notably James Lockyer and Max Gilbert who was first viola in the Boyd Neel Orchestra when I joined later. None of the specialist violists would have dreamt of taking on a violin student. Rowsby didn't have any past reputation for playing the viola, and I never once saw him with the instrument in his hands. Max Gilbert had been in the past a Woof pupil; I have already mentioned Rosemary Green and Stanley Popperwell and now there was Bunty Lempfert who quickly developed into a first class chamber music player, so Woof must have had some way of inspiring young viola players.

I seem to have digressed from the title of this chapter somewhat, to thoughts about various other contemporary students at the Academy, though they all influenced me at the time I was living in the Marlborough Place house. However, apart from the musical influences, the strongest figure having an impact on all the students' lives was certainly the formidably owner and landlady, Mrs. Daisy Tresehar.

All we knew about Daisy was that she had been an actress in London's West End – in what, when, where or with whom we did not know nor dared we ask. She was short, stout, moved like a galleon in full sail. Under an elegant coiffeur of grey hair was a pair of icy blue eyes capable of shattering the self-confidence of anybody who might incur her displeasure. She ruled us with a rod of iron – confiscating our ration books and allowing us the minimum amount at mealtimes to keep body and soul together. From her room at breakfast-time came the appetizing fragrant smell of bacon and eggs, plus, according to our fevered imaginations, luscious mushrooms, tomatoes and sausages, whilst we were lucky to get cornflakes and a thin slice of spam! To be fair to Daisy, you had to have someone with some strength of character to keep all those rowdy young kids in order. I remember one evening we had some sort of cushion fight in the large lounge, largely instigated I seem to remember by my friend John Kirkland in his emancipated days. Someone threw something at me – instead of taking it full in the face I ducked, consequently the cushion hit a rather hideous Victorian vase above the fireplace which fell with a large bang. The door flew open and Daisy stood revealed in her full majesty, radiating displeasure.

"What is going on – what are you doing?"

"Oh, just playing about Mrs. Tresehar" we mumbled.

"Well, don't make such a confounded noise!"

After stony glares all round she withdrew. We were left suitably abashed. I picked up the vase and found to my horror that it had suffered a small hole at one side. We put it back on the mantelpiece with the hole facing the wall and just hoped it wouldn't be noticed.

The sequel to this was that eighteen months later when I was already in the Royal Marines, I arrived in London on leave needing a bed for the night. I turned up at Daisy's and was kindly given a room. After supper I wandered up into the lounge and surreptitiously examined the vase. It was exactly where we had placed it, still with the hole facing the wall, the damage seemingly undiscovered and appearing not to have been moved since, even for such minimum requirements as dusting.

Mrs. Doris Davison was Daisy's side-kick and assistant. She was actually a boarder, but in return for helping out, we surmised that Doris lived there at a reduced rent. She was a more motherly figure than Daisy and helped to alleviate the otherwise authoritarian regime, so the general atmosphere was really very pleasant. Doris knew lots of people in music and in the film world. As I told in the last book, she worked as secretary to Ernest Irving, the well-known conductor and composer of film music who operated mostly at Ealing Studios, and we heard marvelous stories about the goings-on in that, to us, exciting world. Later after the war, when I began to get dates to play in film sessions I was able to experience this for myself at first hand.

I associate Marlborough Place with an every broadening experience of music, both classical and more modern. We listened regularly to the radio installed in our lounge. There were no little transistor sets to have in our rooms in those days, which was an advantage I think, because we were obliged to listen to broadcasts together and often have lively discussions afterwards. The Proms, following the destruction of the old Queens Hall, began again in what is still their venue – the vast Albert Hall. Some of us attended these in person, but mostly we couldn't afford to, so we heard the broadcasts regularly. At this time I began to be fascinated with the music of Sibelius and I remember one year getting familiar with the 1st, 2nd, 3rd, 5th, and 7th Symphonies. The less familiar 4th and 6th have been long neglected, which I think is a shame, because if they were more regularly performed, their less easily understood virtues would be better and more widely appreciated. I have always possessed the scores of all the symphonies and I take every chance to hear them still.

Another composer revealed to me at this time was Bela Bartok. He was then regarded as an extreme avant-garde, and a sure way to empty a concert auditorium was to include a work of his in the programme. Even when I was in Liverpool between 1955 and 1966, to put on the Concerto for Orchestra was a major and rather daring undertaking, requiring lots of extra rehearsals. Nowadays, that marvelous work is more or less standard repertoire, and a good performance will certainly be greeted by any audience with rapturous applause.

In 1941 during my second year at the RAM, I bought the recording by the Hungarian Quartet of Bartok's Fifth String Quartet from the HMV shop in Oxford Street. This was guaranteed to be an authentic performance as the leading violinist was Joseph Székely, friend and close collaborator of the composer. We had a gramophone at Marlborough Place, and I played this wonderful music through and through, absolutely fascinated by its jagged, scintillating rhythms and vividly colourful harmonies. I still think this work is one of the very finest by the great Nationalistic composer.

Further Scrapings

It was of course recorded at that time on the old 78 rpm format, with each side containing just about 4 minutes of music, so it took up three double-sided discs, with the first movement using both sides of the first disc. I was so thrilled with it that as soon as I could I went down to Boosey & Hawkes showrooms in Regent Street and bought the miniature score. Carrying it triumphantly home I put the record on again and tried to follow the music with the score. To my absolute surprise I immediately became completely lost! I tried several times, but always with the same result. The rhythms seemed roughly the same, but the notes were completely different. The explanation that soon emerged was that the record company had stuck the labels of the first disc (containing the first movement) on the wrong sides! The movement is in strict classical sonata form, and I in all innocence had been listening to it from the recapitulation to the end, then turning the disc over and having it played to me from the beginning to the half way mark. To be perfectly honest, it sounded quite reasonable either way!

In those days, with no TV, we listened much more avidly to the radio, which I think for budding musicians was a good thing. Woof used to watch over our development in this way, and taught us a few lessons thereby. I remember one evening we sat round the radio and listened to a performance with the BBC Symphony Orchestra of the Beethoven Violin Concerto with Max Rostal as soloist. The next morning I had a lesson with Woof, and when I entered the room he immediately said

"Boy, did you hear the Beethoven Concerto last night?"

"Yes Sir, I did" I replied.

"What did you think of it?"

"Well – er – I thought it was a bit out of tune!"

He gave me the most awful telling off! "You've no right to talk about a fine player like that. Out of Tune! Out of Tune! What do you think about your intonation? It isn't perfect, is it? No, it certainly isn't! You want to listen to good players and try to learn from them, learn the good things, not always think yourself so clever at finding little faults in them!" He really cut me down to size, and quite rightly so. But I didn't feel too bad afterwards, because he didn't actually say I was wrong, and the performance certainly wasn't perfectly in tune!

I mentioned disappointments, and in student days we certainly got our share of them! As I have said before, it is good to have some disappointments and learn how to deal with them, but I remember one particularly which really made me suffer. When the Henry Wood Prom Concerts were on at the Albert Hall, the Academy occasionally got calls from maybe the BBC, the LSO or the LPO for good students to fill last minute gaps caused by illness. I was once sent down to sit at the back of the first violins in the LSO for a morning rehearsal and a Prom concert the same evening. The conductor was the redoubtable George Szell: then in the early stages of his career he was conductor of the Scottish National Orchestra, but was booked for this guest engagement with the LSO. The main work was Richard Strauss "*Don Juan*". I had never heard of the piece, much less played it. Szell took it at a virtuosic pace which quite frankly frightened the pants off me! I was sitting with a little elderly desk partner who I could tell was not all that good, but he seemed to know how to cope with it. I was completely flummoxed at not being able to play every note, and felt I was a complete failure. I rushed home to Marlborough Place, charged up into my Muriel's room, and burst into tears! I would never be good enough to play in an orchestra and so on and so on! She very sensibly gave me a good cuddle, and slowly the pain eased. For someone completely inexperienced, it is really intimidating to sit at the back of a large section in the vast Albert Hall acoustics. You feel as if you are completely alone, and that everyone in the audience can hear every note of your pathetic scrabbling. Now of course, I have learnt how to cope with such things. Actually, "Don Juan" is not as unplayable as it first seems, and a competent orchestral violinist does actually play pretty well all the notes. But you learn over the years how to present the essentials of what can be the outrageous demands of some composers. If the music is truly impossible to play, it will also be impossible to hear, so your job is to present the sound which gives the nearest impression of what the composer in his little ivory tower has written!

Chapter 9 – The War

Looking back on the six years between the outbreak of war on 3rd September 1939 and the final Japanese surrender on 2nd September 1945, what often strikes me is that within this comparatively short space of time, such a vast panorama of events managed to have been packed in; both for me personally and for the country at large.

From my own personal standpoint it included one year at school, almost three complete years as a student, and over two years in the Royal Marines. It took me from being a sixteen year old schoolboy to being a twenty-two year old married man. It included one long year of adolescence, followed by the London Blitz which marked the start of three years of concentrated work to transform me from a potential musician into one who had gained the professional equipment needed for a career in music. Then there was the experience of being suddenly plunged into the alien life of the army, including participation in the Second Front and being one of the first British troops to enter into Paris. Finally there was marriage and the beginning of the Far East Tour with the Marine Band. It was not until December 1947 after two frustrating post-war years that I was able to leave the Marines, so my spell in the Forces lasted over four years altogether.

It is difficult to believe that all this could have been encapsulated into such a relatively brief span of time. Remembering back to each phase, they all seemed to last interminably. I suppose the reason for this is that we can recall the immediate past but we can't foresee the future. During the bombing of London, the grim routine of air-raid sirens and broken nights' sleep felt it had been going on for ever, and one couldn't see any reason for it to cease. Yet, after about seven months, the worst was over. On 10th May 1941 the Luftwaffe destroyed the Houses of Parliament, but on the same day Rudolf Hess flew to Britain, presumably with some proposal for peace, of which we will never know the details. Germany began to be increasingly involved on the Russian Front, and to some extent the pressure on us was off.

Further Scrapings

The war did, however, seem to enter a phase in which good news was scarce and time hung heavily. There was a period during that summer term when German bombers mounted daylight raids on London – not so ferociously as the previous autumn, but enough to cause concern. The attacks were so sporadic that the air raid sirens were no real guide as to whether danger was actually imminent, so most London buildings had a system of Roof Spotters who rang down when they judged something might happen. I remember one hot, overcast Thursday afternoon when the First Orchestra was rehearsing with Sir Henry Wood. The work was Tschaikovsky's Nutcracker Suite. The sirens had sounded during lunchtime, but we started anyway and ploughed hopefully through the March - Overture. Right on the final chord, the bells rang and we trooped down obediently to the basement. A cup of tea and a quarter of an hour later we were allowed up, and tinkled our way through the Dance of the Sugar Plum Fairy. Fortunately this is only a couple of minutes long, because we were again interrupted and bidden to the basement. This happened several times – never once did we manage more than one complete movement. I seem to remember that before we managed to get to the last of the eight movements, the Waltz of the Flowers, Sir Henry sent us all home in despair!

That year did however see the event which probably guaranteed the eventual victory of the Allies, though there was still much tribulation and disappointment to come. Again, it is something which is associated in my mind with a particular place. On the 7th December 1941 I was well into my second complete year at the Academy. For some reason I remember myself outside St Pancras Station – perhaps I was enquiring about trains to take me home for the Christmas holidays. Be that as it may, I can see as clearly as in a photograph the Evening Standard posters –"JAPANESE BOMB PEARL HARBOUR - USA ENTERS THE WAR". Just to say or to think those words flashes up in my mind a clear picture of the beautiful Pugin façade of the station, bathed in the pale winter sunshine of that momentous day. That news meant that we were no longer alone. Everybody felt that sense of relief. We knew that Roosevelt had been on our side, but now he would be able to bring the whole of the USA behind us. The actual event of course was a disaster, with lives lost, ships and planes destroyed, and indeed it was followed by much more bad news. On 15th February 1942 Singapore fell to the Japanese, on the 19th, they bombed the city of Darwin in Australia. The Americans suffered many reverses in the Pacific, but slowly began to hit back. 18th April saw USA Flying Fortresses dropping bombs on Tokyo, and eventually, much to our relief we began to hear better news from our Forces in the Middle East.

2nd October 1942 brought the first British counter attack at El Alamein. Churchill had appointed General Bernard Montgomery in command of North Africa. He was an uncompromising character, not always loved by his fellow officers, but followed unquestioningly by the troops, and by the public. Gerry MacDonald, who was later manager of the Royal Liverpool Philharmonic when I was there, was serving with the Desert Rats in North Africa at the time. He used to tell us how Monty would get a couple of hundred men round him in the middle of the desert and give a demonstration of how it was possible to clean your teeth, shave and have a complete wash down, stripping off completely, with one mug full of precious water. Probably you had to drink what was left! Things like that really endeared him to the rank and file – he knew how to communicate. Gerald himself as a manager was quite the best I have known at keeping up the morale of an orchestra, and maybe he learnt that skill to some extent from Montgomery. The Desert Army under Monty, with his characteristic beret, defeated Rommel on 4th November of that year, and this was without doubt one of the most decisive moments of the War. Gradually the momentum grew, though it was a long, bitter struggle, which we at home watched often apprehensively.

Unlike the First War, this conflict did not have the same insatiable thirst for cannon fodder which characterized the dreadful trench warfare of Northern France. When I became liable to conscription, I was advised by the Academy to apply for deferral until the summer of 1943 so that I could complete my three year course. This was granted quite easily by an appearance before a magistrate in Marylebone. It was against a background of hard but sure and steady progress by our troops across North Africa and up into Italy, that I was enabled to work during the next year to justify this chance I had been given. I remember, those of us studying in the Academy at that time regretting that we did not have the opportunities which might have been open in peacetime for young players to continue with post-graduate work either in Europe or America, but in spite of that, those wartime years did produce a good crop of musicians who I am convinced have enriched Britain's musical life in the second half of the 20th century.

Chapter 10 – The Royal Marines Band, Plymouth Division

In times of war, many musicians feel apprehensive at the risk to the hands and fingers of army activities. The loss of one finger, whilst not vitally important in many professions, could be the end for a violinist or pianist, so we who depend for a living on manipulating hands and fingers tend to avoid more violent sports like rugby, and likewise are especially fearful of any other dangerous vigorous activity. Many musicians in both world wars found the opportunity to serve in army bands, and in the last war, the Royal Air Force Band based in Uxbridge absorbed many of the finest London musicians. This included the great horn player Dennis Brain, violinists Fred Grinke (my teacher), David Martin, Leonard Hirsch, Harry Blech, violist Max Gilbert, cellist James Whitehead, the Griller String Quartet, pianist Dennis Matthews and many others.

I never actually heard the orchestra that was formed from the wartime members of the RAF Band, but to judge from the pedigree of its members, it must have been a fabulous ensemble. Dennis Brain was certainly the greatest horn player this country has ever produced, and was also a wonderful all-round musician. I was privileged to play in the Philharmonia from 1950 to 1955 when he was first horn, and it was a devastating tragedy when he was killed in a motor accident on September 1st 1957. Sitting with him as second horn, in the RAF and in the Philharmonia was Norman Del Mar, who was destined to make his mark as a fine conductor. He was first encouraged to conduct by Sir Thomas Beecham, and quickly made his name as a most efficient and knowledgeable musician. I worked with him many times – most notably when he was chief conductor of the BBC Training Orchestra. One of his legacies is the three volume publication devoted to the life and music of Richard Strauss. Fred Grinke, Canadian violinist, was one of the greatest students of Rowsby Woof, and when Woof died I was lucky enough to be able to continue lessons with him. As I have written earlier, he was leader of the Boyd Neel Orchestra and virtually launched my career by offering me a position in it. David

Martin, quartet leader and soloist, gained an equal reputation as a teacher to Grinke, and married the fine cellist and teacher Florence Hooton. Leonard Hirsch was also a fine quartet leader, and was for a time leader of the Philharmonia. Harry Blech, another great quartet leader became better known as conductor of the London Mozart Players which he founded. Max Gilbert later led the violas in the Boyd Neel Orchestra, and James Whitehead also led the cellos. Jimmy was much in demand post war as a concerto soloist. James Merret, double bass, was also in the RAF Band, and he in turn migrated later to lead his section in the Philharmonia. In fact, Walter Legge who was the ruthless founder of that orchestra drew very heavily on ex members of the RAF for his original group. To finish the roster, the Griller Quartet was absorbed into Uxbridge as a complete unit. They were our finest chamber ensemble at the time and were thus enabled to continue their musical development undisturbed into the post war years. The same can be said for Dennis Matthews, not only one of Britain's finest pianists at the time, but also a musicologist of quite phenomenal erudition.

When I was eventually called up, there were no more vacancies at Uxbridge, so my family urged me to take the chance to join the Royal Marine Band in Plymouth. I had actually heard the Band play on the radio, and had been greatly impressed by the Toscanini-like brio and precision they produced under the remarkable Colonel Kenneth Ricketts. When I mentioned this to a piano student at the Academy who was actually his daughter, she said her father was looking for someone to lead their Symphony Orchestra, so it was arranged that I should accept that position.

The Royal Marines had three Divisions based in Portsmouth, Plymouth and Chatham. Each of these had a Divisional Band which was required to provide music for ceremonial parades and also orchestras and dance bands for troop entertainment. Membership of these was mostly confined to regulars, men who were making the service their career. What is called the Royal Marine School of Music generally provided bands for service on ships, such as aircraft carriers and large battleships. There was a certain amount of interchange between these two, but generally the Divisional Bands provided all the music for land-based ceremonies and musical activities. However, during the war and the immediate aftermath, the big Divisional Bands were used for visits abroad and for playing to troops in the war areas. I have written previously about the Plymouth Band's involvement in the Normandy invasion, and that we were also the first British troops to enter Paris, just behind the American battalions. We also formed part of the large combined Band and Orchestra which toured the Far East attached to Lord Mountbatten, celebrating his re-instatement to Singapore immediately after the defeat of Japan. But there were other trips abroad which we made in the aftermath of the liberation of Europe, notably a visit to Holland in 1956.

This was the first time we could realize a little of what things must have been like in Europe under the Nazi yoke. Our time in Normandy had been spent billeted in remote farmhouses, sleeping in barns, and we had little contact with the population at large. In Paris the atmosphere was of a huge party, celebrating the liberation, and thankful that the Germans had spared the city from devastation. But in Amsterdam and Rotterdam we could hear more of the actual suffering that had been endured.

We were put up in ordinary households, which only a few weeks before had been homes for German troops. Of course, many of them had behaved perfectly well, but the terrible things that were allowed to take place in some instances were shocking to hear. The Dutch are traditionally good English speakers, and so we had many heart-rending stories told directly to us. An example which I never will forget is the couple who told us that they were on a crowded bus in Rotterdam with their ten year old little boy. He accidentally trod on the toe of a Gestapo officer, and wouldn't apologize. The child was taken away and the parents were told to come to the army headquarters next day to collect him. They did so – but on arrival they were coolly informed that the boy was dead! Things like this, which were not uncommon, produced the virulent hatred of the Germans, which must have taken many years post war to disperse. We felt thankful that our island status had at least protected us from this kind of suffering. I am sure we now realize that Germans are not on average any more or less ruthless and cruel than other nationalities, but when a party such as the Nazis, with an amoral, gangster-like mentality gains control, the worst tendencies of everyone are released, and are allowed to become permissive, normal practice

As the first British musicians to visit the country since before the War, we were given a warm welcome everywhere, even giving concerts in the famous Concertgebouw hall in Amsterdam. We also visited Rotterdam and other towns, but I'm afraid my memories are unclear about further locations. We were doing much more parades and ceremonial occasions, and not so many concerts. However, I still remember the friendliness of the Dutch people, and have always been happy to revisit the country several times in later life.

Back in England I began a time of increasing frustration. Looking back, I can see my time in the Marines was in many ways a good experience. I enjoyed many friendships and horizons were certainly widened considerably, but at the time it was horribly frustrating to feel that all my musical studies were being wasted. Colonel Ricketts, who had originally invited me to join, had told me that I would have to sign on in the Marines for twelve years, which I did, but only after he had assured me confidently that I would be allowed to buy my discharge whenever the War should end. Unfortunately, one year later he retired, and shortly afterwards he died. His successor, Lieutenant Stoner, completely refused to allow me to ask for release from the Forces, thus confirming the famous quote of the Hollywood film magnate Sam Goldwyn – "A verbal contract isn't worth the paper it's written on". Instead of joining all my contemporaries in rebuilding a career in the exciting post-war London musical scene, I seemed doomed to a further nine years isolated in Plymouth, with the highlight of my existence as a violinist being the chance to play Monti's Czardas at the weekly officers' Mess Night dinners in Stonehouse Barracks. Fortunately liberation was at hand, as I have described more fully in my previous book, in the shape of H. M. Medland, the Labour MP for Plymouth. He heard me play at a concert in the town and suggested that Muriel, my wife, should write to him detailing all aspects of my case, as members of the Forces were absolutely forbidden to approach a member of parliament. To cut a long story short, this she did, and after what seemed an interminable silence, in December 1957 I suddenly received the best Christmas present of my life – freedom from the Marines!

Chapter 11 – London 1948 to 1955

For anyone starting out in a career in music, whatever the particular circumstances of the time, it is very likely that they will go through a period of struggle and uncertainty. Muriel and I certainly did, and the things that got us through were our love of each other, our love of music and of the variety and stimulation of the musical scene at the time. Also, this period saw the birth of our first two children – Paul in 1949 and Alison in 1954, which was a great joy and kept us busy!

Our position and prospects outwardly seemed good. I had already been playing in the Boyd Neel Orchestra whenever I could get leave from the Marine Band, and now I could become a full time member of what was the most prestigious chamber orchestra in the country. I was having some lessons with Fred Grinke the leader, and then I began studying with Sascha Lasserson which gave a great lift to my playing and prospects. Muriel was doing quite a lot of work for CEMA[9] and having been teaching in the Junior School at the RAM she was now appointed as a full professor. She also worked with the London Opera School which gave her great pleasure as she always loved accompanying singers for which she had a natural aptitude.

However, the Boyd Neel work, although wonderfully satisfying, did not have the continuity of engagements that orchestras such as the LSO, LPO and indeed the BBC Orchestras had. Often a month or more would go by with no work with the BN at all, so I had to rely to a large extent on free-lance work, which only gradually began to build up. Much juggling of the diary was needed. You had not only to develop a reputation as a good player, but also a reliable person so that the "fixers"[10] would continue to ring you up.

When we were married in 1945, we had managed to rent a small two-room first-floor flat at 130, King Henry's Road, not far from Swiss Cottage, North-West London. This was comfortable enough, convenient for the time being, and was the best we could afford in those early days. However, it quickly became more and more restrictive. When Paul arrived on the scene, things were really chaotic, pulling prams up and down the stairs, and having the baby sleeping every night in our bedroom. Broken nights, together with the need to practice, and arranging complicated routines for babysitters and domestic helps all in two rooms was enough to bring on several nervous breakdowns. We had a lovely Irish girl living in Kilburn who traveled over several times a week to help us out. I remember Muriel saying to her once – "Ah Ellen, You must think we're all completely mad here!" To which she immediately replied in her lovely Irish accent– "Oh well, I'm sure it's very nice, Madame".

At this time, Muriel's mother moved to London from Coventry and came to stay with us. This was meant to enable us both to do our professional work and she would be able to look after Paul. It just didn't work. When we were all three at home plus the baby in such a small space, tensions inevitably became acute. Isobel (Muriel's mother) was sleeping on an uncomfortable sofa in our living room, and being exasperatingly uncomplaining and self sacrificing about it. We all had to go to bed at the same time. Her ideas of what was good for Paul were not always mine, and Muriel was torn between us. It was impossible. So eventually we managed to find an even smaller flat for her in FitzJohns Avenue, about half a mile away. Then she could visit us and help out when needed, but we could have more time to ourselves which reduced tensions considerably. I remember we eventually put Paul to sleep in the bathroom, and he loved it! We had the almost forgotten luxury of a few unbroken nights' sleep.

We gradually got more work, felt financially a bit more stable, and in late 1952 were able to afford the rent of an entire house at number 92 in the same road, much nearer to Chalk Farm station. Although somewhat ramshackle, this was better from every point of view. We were just near Primrose Hill, and Muriel when she was teaching at the RAM could walk there over the Hill, past London Zoo and across Regents Park to York Gate where the Academy lies, through lovely greenery the whole way. Pushing a pram around there was good fun, crossing over into the Park and circumnavigating the Zoological Gardens, where Paul in his push chair could easily see a whole line of various species – Okapi, Antelopes, and Gazelles all had their enclosures freely visible from Regents Park. We called this the Free Zoo! We really loved the area and it was good not to move away from it. King Henry's Road is built directly over the railway tunnel for the mainline Euston trains, so it felt familiar that in the new home we had the same rattling of the glassware in our kitchen cupboard every time an express accelerated fiercely northwards out of the station.

It was from 92 King Henry's Road that we witnessed the coronation of Queen, Elizabeth II on 2nd June 1953. As always gadget mad, I had managed to install a new-fangled TV set in our lounge, and all our neighbours came in to see it. Also, we heard about the conquest of Everest by Edmund Hillary and Sherpa Tensing – it was an exciting time for the country. We watched the whole of the Coronation, beautifully filmed by the BBC, and had a large celebratory meal. That evening it seemed the thing to do to go into the centre of the city and see the celebrations at first hand. So, Muriel and Paul (aged four) with a friend piled into our tiny Renault 4CV car and set off. Imagine the traffic congestion on that momentous day. We struggled down as far as Trafalgar Square and turned into Whitehall, when the traffic finally stuck and we were immovable. My dear Muriel responded to the situation with one of her more priceless remarks – "Well darling, I think we've seen enough. I think we'll go home now!" I don't know what she expected me to do. Perhaps marital confidence credited me with possession of a magic wand! In the event, we did get home about three hours later.

We had the space to invite friends and colleagues for meals and parties, and the area was home to many musicians that we worked with. We let out a large front room to a Scottish singer, Niven Miller, and he ran a very good madrigal group which used to rehearse there under the direction of Imogen Holst, the composer Gustav Holst's daughter, who also became a kind of amanuensis to Benjamin Britten. She was an incredibly lively and energetic musician – almost overpowering in her enthusiasms. I later played in several recording sessions for EMI at Abbey Road that she conducted with the English Chamber Orchestra of her father's music. I thought of her as a kind of English version of Nadia Boulanger, the great French musicologist and teacher, who often conducted the Boyd Neel.

The big worry, then as now, for musicians living in crowded environments, was the need to practice and rehearse, and the impact of this on neighbours. We had a fair amount of trouble with this in our first small flat at number 130, but eventually got some sort of agreement with the people around us. If we were reasonable about not making music too late in the evening, the people next door gradually became more tolerant. It was strange to find that if we were playing fairly regularly during normal daytime hours the complaints died down. If, however, for whatever reason, we were away for two or three weeks, when we returned, as soon as we played the first few notes the complaints started again in full force. In our small accommodation, we had strangers to the left and the right, above and below, which to say the least was difficult. The piano, sitting firmly on the floor, was most annoying for people below, whilst those upstairs suffered more from the violin. We were much luckier in our new home at number 92 as it was semi detached. We had a semi basement kitchen area together with a nice garden room, and on the main floor above a very pleasant large music room. The one adjoining room next door was occupied by a rather eccentric elderly gentleman who was slightly deaf. He used to complain that if he had to hear music he preferred to be able to hear what it was, so would we please play louder!

Life in this cosmopolitan area was very pleasant at that time, and we were both doing more and more rewarding work, financially and musically. We liked to describe the area as South Hampstead, but in reality it was Chalk Farm – not nearly so posh. However, there was the advantage that Chalk Farm Road, leading down to Camden Town, contained a wealth of antique shops and second-hand furniture stores that were a delight to browse through, and we bought a variety of items which added to the atmosphere of our enlarged accommodation at number 92; some of which I still have.

Chapter 12 – Cars

In the early fifties, the idea of owning a car became more and more of an obsession with us young players. The post war economy was only very slowly improving, and getting a new or fairly new vehicle was an impossible dream. On the other hand, having a car meant that it was easier to get about between various free-lance dates[11], and parking was nowhere near the problem that it became later. You used to be able to drive down for a day's sessions at Kingsway Hall and find a space fairly easily just outside the beautiful Freemasons Hall building in Great Queen Street, or alternatively across Kingsway in Lincoln's Inn Fields; quite impossible today, what with soaring meter costs and the Congestion Charge.

Our first car, bought in I think 1950, from a chap who had a scruffy little back-street garage near the BBC Studios in Maida Vale, was a rather fabulous Talbot 75 saloon, dating from 1933. It was pretty decrepit, and broke down on numerous occasions, but my little garage man (I wish I could remember his name) always managed to repair it at minimum expense. It was an impressive beast, and when it was going (!) was a real pleasure to drive. A pre-selector gearbox, worked from a quadrant lever on the steering column provided immaculate gearshifts. The mechanism was superbly engineered and was in fact almost the only part of the car that never gave any trouble. It was quite a luxury vehicle and had several ingenious devices that appealed to my love of gadgets. Instead of a winding mechanism for the driver's window it had a foot-long lever working on a ratchet that when you pushed it down, opened the heavy plate-glass window in one smooth swoop. Ideal in the days when you were supposed to give constant hand signals.

I took my road test in it, in Hendon. This lever came in useful then, because I remember that the first words the examiner said to me were -

"Mr. Mountain, I want you to give hand signals exclusively during this test."

I replied, trying to be a bit clever

"Er – what if I need to signal to traffic behind me to the left?"

Back came a brusque reply "I'm not here to tell you how to drive!"

I thought to myself – O my God, we've got a miserable old so-and-so here. I set off in grim silence, determined to get the better of him. Everything went fine, though I was a bit tense and nervy. However, disaster soon struck. Whilst turning right in front of some oncoming traffic, I managed to stall the engine. I immediately thought – that's the end – I've failed. So, feeling quite resigned, I calmly started up and drove on without saying a word.

At the end, the examiner said -

"Well, Mr. Mountain, I'm passing you for this test. You drove mainly well enough. Unfortunately you did manage to stall the car once, but it didn't seem to upset you; you managed the whole thing calmly, which was good!"

I often quote this little incident to pupils, to illustrate that one little mistake is not important – more important is the way you deal with it.

The final incident in the Talbot saga came in 1952. Muriel and I were getting quite a lot of sonata recital dates in various parts of the country, and on this occasion we drove down to East Grinstead to play for the local Music Club. Everything seemed to be going well – the old banger had been just serviced and was spinning along as sweet as a nut. The Secretary greeted us outside the hall and asked me to park inside the gates, which I did. Just before I turned off the engine there was a sudden almighty clonk, and the whole car became completely immobile. The big end had gone, and there was no way we could drive back. After the concert we returned home on a Green Line bus and left our poor old Talbot to the tender mercies of a local garage. The sequel was that my friend and colleague Arthur Davison, violinist and later conductor, who was with me in the Philharmonia at the time was then living not far from East Grinstead and after prolonged negotiations I sold it to him for £25, payable in five monthly installments of £5. He had the car repaired, and it served him and his family excellently for about four years![12]

Our next car was a complete contrast. After driving about in a sort of family-sized limousine, I managed to get hold of a much more modern Renault 4CV, which was in very good condition, only a couple of years old and a very smart sky blue colour. It had a rear engine like a Volkswagen and was also roughly the same shape as the German car, only smaller. It was ideal for London traffic and parking, and for a time we really enjoyed it. It was much more reliable than the ancient old Talbot, and that was a great relief. However, we quickly found that it was horribly cramped for any trips with the baby, and luggage space was pretty limited; the front boot contained the spare wheel, leaving room for one small suitcase. Also, it wasn't very stable. I had one very nervy moment with it, coming home on a drizzly autumn evening. Driving up Park Road from Baker Street to the west of Regents Park, you come to a roundabout which leads on past Lords cricket ground to St Johns Wood. Incredibly enough, this roundabout used to be paved with wooden blocks. They were smooth enough in normal conditions, but if there was a slight shower just after a dry spell they were treacherous. I drove around at a normal brisk speed when suddenly there was absolutely no control. The little Renault spun like a top, and I found myself facing completely the wrong way. I think autumn leaves on top of the greasy wet wood might have been to blame. Fortunately I didn't hit anything, but I crept home in third gear, feeling pretty shaken, and planning another change of vehicle.

Hans Geiger, my much respected colleague in the Philharmonia violins, a bachelor with no family to support and an obsession with motoring, had recently acquired an almost new Jowett Javelin which was his pride and joy, also the envy of all the rest of us. When I found another Javelin, a bit older, for sale in a Hampstead garage, I immediately began to try to organize the cash for its purchase, not only just to keep up with Hans, my friendly rival, but of course because the firm that produced it was Jowett of Bradford, my home town.[13]

The Jowett Javelin was an award-winning British car that was produced from 1947 to 1953 by Jowett of Bradford. The car was designed by Gerald Palmer during World War II and was intended to be a major leap forward following the rather staid designs of pre-war Jowetts. It had a maximum speed of 77 mph and a 0-50 mph time of 13.4 seconds. Two Zenith carburettors were fitted and PA and PB versions had hydraulic tappets. The radiator was behind the engine. A four speed gearbox with column change was used. An early example won the Monte Carlo Rally of 1949 whilst another came first in the 2-litre touring-car class at the Spa 24-hour race that same year. The 1952 International RAC Rally was won by a Javelin which also took the Best Closed Car award, while the 1953 International Tulip Rally was won outright by a privately entered Javelin. So, for its time, this was a pretty sporty family saloon. The only snag was that due to the very forward situation of the engine, in front of the radiator, in excessively rainy weather water came through the front grille onto the plugs and the car stopped. You just had to wait patiently and let the engine heat dry them out. This defect had been rectified in Hans's model, but mine occasionally succumbed to it. However, on the whole, it was a good car, way ahead of its time, and gave us many miles of satisfying motoring.

In my previous book I mention the second European Tour with Karajan in October 1954, when a number of orchestral members elected to go by private transport. These were mainly violinists, and if the cars had not made it to any particular concert, the orchestra would have been minus practically all the first fiddles, including the leader! Manoug was driving his smart 2.5 Riley with Bill Kerr and two others, Hans Geiger in his Javelin had Jessie Hinchliffe, Jack Kessler and another I can't remember, and I, in my Javelin, had Marie Wilson, Ernest Scott and Derek Collier – twelve first violins in all. Jane Withers, Walter Legge's assistant and the orchestral manager, tried hard to stop us, but we stuck it out, and I think we got away with it because Karajan was a keen driver and rather admired us for doing so. In the event, we were on time for every rehearsal and concert, and on several occasions the rest of the band were late, due to train delays.

Further Scrapings

I must say it was a pretty gruelling undertaking, but great fun. The early concerts were for the Aix-en-Provence Festival, and we did an open air concert at Les Baux de Provence, the beautiful village and fabulous ruined fortress that is a must-see tourist attraction in the area. Karajan hated the whole event. He obviously thought it demeaning to have to play outdoors, and conducted throughout with his eyes shut, making his disapproval as clear as possible. Halfway through the second movement of Berlioz Symphonie Fantastique the hot Mediterranean *Mistral* wind sprang up and swept most of the violin section's music off the stands; he ignored this completely, shutting his eyes even tighter!.

The orchestra had previously dined well in the beautiful restaurants in the village, so we were all in a pretty light-hearted mood, and didn't take that particular concert too seriously. The mood had previously been set at the beginning when Jock Sutcliffe, our wonderful oboist, stood up to give the A, and presaged it with the first two bars of "Jingle Bells"!

That afternoon, a crowd of us had gone into a rather posh hotel which had a large swimming pool. We all wanted a swim, but I unfortunately didn't have a bathing costume with me. A lady who was part of the management of the Festival said "O, a friend might be able to help you." I was led across to the far side of the pool, and the friend turned out to be none other than Lord Harewood, a regular visitor to international music festivals. I had the honour of using the bathing trunks, if only the second best ones, of a cousin of the Queen!

Our journey down through Italy took in one rather provincial concert in Perugia, which confirmed to us the widely-held belief that typical Italian audiences are entirely focussed on vocal music, and purely instrumental performances leave them cold. Berlioz, in his wonderful "Memoirs" makes clear that he believed this to be true, and we were witness to the fact that in some cases it still is. Karajan conducted our concert in Perugia's Teatro Communale. The programme was received in a rather lukewarm manner, and some members of the audience could be heard chatting volubly whilst the music was being played. The second half was devoted entirely to Beethoven

3rd Symphony, the "*Eroica*". It was evident that the concert-goers of Perugia were finding the whole thing rather boring, and things came to a head when at one point in the last movement, where there is a pause on the dominant chord, an imperfect cadence with obviously more to come, they all burst into applause – thinking (or rather hoping!) that it was all over. We really expected Karajan to stalk off the platform in silent protest, but he held on manfully and finished the performance with a grim visage.

The Jowett Javelin served us admirably on this long and testing journey, but when we got down to Naples, it obviously needed a full service and a few minor repairs. We left it in a garage to have the work done and boarded the ferry to Sicily for a concert in Palermo. I had left detailed instructions with the manager who spoke reasonable English, and arranged to pick it up four days later. Imagine my horror when we found on our return that nothing had been done – it was still standing, very travel-worn, in the exact corner of the forecourt where I had left it. Consternation! The manager was called. He had a raging row with the head mechanic, in screaming Italian, each blaming the other. Marie couldn't stand it any longer and burst into tears. The sight of a lady in distress went straight to the hearts of the sentimental Neapolitans. The whole garage stopped all other work and concentrated on putting our steed into first rate order, and in little over two hours we were on the road.

Our troubles were not really over, however. We had watched the other cars go speeding past and we were well over two hours behind. It was by now late morning, and we had to be in Turin, over 550 miles away, for rehearsal and concert the next day. This was well before the advent of motorways, and you just drove right through the centre of every town and village. In any case, the Jowett, although very much a state-of-the-art car of its day, had a top speed rated at only 77 mph. I am quite proud of the fact that I drove the whole journey myself, including about 100 miles of thick fog between Genoa and Turin. We arrived at our hotel just after 1 am, and turned up for the rehearsal next morning, putting a brave face on things and managing to look reasonably refreshed!

Driving in those days was all a bit of an adventure. I look back on that period in London with those three cars with nostalgia, and later motoring days seem to be much more utilitarian and boring, so I propose to end the car saga for the present, and before passing on to Liverpool days, to recall some more details of free-lance work in London before 1955.

Chapter 13 – A Time of Change

Professional musicians in London, up to the immediate post-war years, seemed to exhibit a curious dichotomy in the appreciation of their own worth. On the one hand, they were acutely conscious of the superiority of standards they felt they had over all provincial musicians. When in 1955 I got the job as leader in Liverpool, many friends were horrified that I should even consider leaving London. Nothing artistically worthwhile could be thought to exist north of Watford. Yet, at the same time, there was the ever present prejudice that anything foreign, be it orchestras, conductors, soloists, must by definition be better than home-grown products. During the War, Ida Handel (a supreme artist by any standards) was living in London, and played regularly with all our best orchestras. I heard her many times in those days. But there were some who denigrated her efforts, saying she only succeeded because there were no visiting violinists from the Continent for her to compete with.

Many were quick to point out that music was subsidized much more lavishly, particularly in Germany, and this was (and still is) true, in spite of the fact that Germany is supposed to have lost the war. Foreign orchestras had better salaries, and much more generous rehearsal time. This again was, and is so, and for these reasons the standard of music abroad was assumed to be always higher. But on the other hand, lots of rehearsal time can often lead to laziness, and British orchestras have a proud reputation of being the finest sight-readers in the world. Nothing is more frustrating to good competent players than having to rehearse unnecessarily. The rare occasions when you have a genius on the box and it is a revelation and a pleasure to work for any length of time are sadly outnumbered by hours when you are being told what you already know by people who themselves know very little. To be fair, we must admit that the situation is mostly somewhere between these two extremes, but with the phenomenal rise in the standards of orchestral playing, the wise conductor these days sees himself as a leader amongst equals rather than an old-fashioned musical dictator.

Further Scrapings

Gradually, during these few years after the war, the self-respect of British musicians began to burgeon. In 1951 the Festival of Britain gave us a first class musical venue beside the Thames – the Royal Festival Hall. Walter Legge was revealing the Philharmonia as an orchestra of international distinction. I was by then a full member of it, and during the opening week of the Hall we played concerts there, including one memorable evening when we were conducted by Vaughan Williams. The other London bands began to follow our lead, and soon London's orchestras were all of international standard. Boyd Neel's orchestra played its part in improving the level of string playing. We began to enjoy visits from the greatest international figures, though it must be said that we also had visits from some foreign musicians of lesser ability who made us realize that not all that glitters from afar is pure gold![14] Visiting conductors, accustomed to the standards of Berlin and Vienna, began to realize that we were no longer (and probably never had been) Das Land Ohne Musik(The Land Without Music). England had always produced fine singers, but the emergence of such a figure as Kathleen Ferrier really shook the international scene, when she was taken up by Bruno Walter to record Mahler's "Song of the Earth". What a tremendous musical asset we lost with that great artist's early death – similarly tragic as the demise of the unique horn player Dennis Brain.

Maybe the single greatest figure in Britain's musical resurgence in the Fifties was provided by a composer. It was realized that our country could produce a musician without peer throughout the 20th century, and indeed throughout the world. What had Germany to put beside Benjamin Britten? Nobody. Here was a musician at least as great in many peoples' eyes, as Shostakovich, Stravinsky, and any other you care to mention. I feel a tremendous honour to have known Britten and to have worked with him on many occasions.

The post war period also marked the virtual beginnings of public subsidy for the Arts, which really started in 1940 when government began to think that artistic activity could play a vital part in strengthening public morale.

The Arts Council of Great Britain was the post-war descendant of the Committee for the Encouragement of Music and the Arts

(CEMA), which was formally set up by Royal Charter in 1940. The Arts Council was established and incorporated by Royal Charter in 1946.

CEMA was a scheme to improve national morale during wartime, as well as an attempt to provide employment for artists, whose usual opportunities were reduced by the effects of war. When the war came to an end, there was still a clear need for the arts to be made more accessible to the general public.

Whereas CEMA was heavily involved in providing arts directly, through promoting theatre and concert tours, the arrival of the Arts Council of Great Britain marked a reduction in direct provision, instead giving more of these responsibilities to individual arts organizations. The objectives of the Arts Council were to assist and encourage

- The improvement of professional standards of performance
- Selective distribution of arts throughout the country
- Local responsibility for promoting theatres, concerts, galleries, arts centres and festivals
- The provision of buildings for arts activities

The Arts Council was responsible to, and financed by, the Treasury through grant-in-aid. It was not a government department; no minister directed its policies or decided to whom funding should be awarded. This arm's length principle – which still exists to some extent today – meant that while the Arts Council had the freedom to make individual funding decisions without intervention from government, it had to be prepared to account for these decisions to government, parliament and the public.

My wife Muriel and I benefited considerably from this. During the war, CEMA had helped to establish a network of Music Clubs throughout the country, and they helped organize tours for young artists like ourselves. They would arrange meetings in various parts of the country to which Club secretaries and officials would be

Further Scrapings

invited, and at which players like us would give a mini recital and have the chance to show our wares, as it were, to the people who could give us work. These were known in our circles as the Arts Council Slave Markets, but they certainly did a good job, and "Peter Mountain and Angela Dale" (Muriel's stage name) were able to develop a countrywide reputation. Muriel also had joined the Judy Hill Piano Trio, with two really outstanding artists; Judy Hill, violin and Olga Hegedus, cello. They were also getting good Arts Council dates, so Muriel was fully occupied. There were occasions when for one reason or another Judy was not free to do concerts, so I was sometimes able to step into the gap. The ensemble then, instead of a Hill had a Mountain!

It is sad that over the years, many of the wartime Music Clubs have sunk into decline, and often just ceased to exist. Often it was because a really live-wire secretary or organizer left and a successor didn't emerge. The few that survive have been remarkable success stories. I am thinking particularly of examples such as Ilkley Concert Club. We did a couple of recitals there shortly after the War, and I think the Trio played there too. Now they have a devoted following with packed audiences at every concert, and programmes given by the foremost artists and chamber groups. It is impossible to get into a concert unless you can obtain a ticket from one of the regular subscribers, and there is a waiting list for season tickets. Societies like these (and there are a significant network throughout the country) do a good job and give satisfaction to a devoted following. But today, with more and more people buying CDs of the greatest performers available, these clubs know they will not continue to prosper unless they provide concerts by established artists and groups well known to their patrons, and through good audience management they have the funds to do this. What we now lack is a body of concert promoters and audiences willing to set their sights a little lower and support up-and-coming young players who need performance experience. Also, by the way, they should be willing to support more enterprising and adventurous programmes, because you can be pretty sure that in the big-time music clubs, the music played will be pretty conventional. The organizers don't want to frighten away their generally well-off and conventional patrons who "know what they like". The wartime

Peter Mountain

and immediately post-war music societies were not so big-time, and were welcoming to young talent, and I must say, to enterprising programmes. We played a lot of contemporary music in our concerts in those days, and got good responses. And, we were fortunate to get the experience that every musician needs, of playing in public and getting the music across to what might be described as average audiences.

This reminds me of an occasion in about 1987, when we were on holiday, motor caravanning down the coastline of what was then Yugoslavia. I remember we spent an evening in the town of Split, and saw advertised a Classical Music Concert in the local hall. We paid and went in, and found an audience, quite a proportion being British, composed almost entirely of holiday tourists. Bargain package holidays to Yugoslavia were very much the thing in those days – cheap and attracting mostly a public to whom the height of classical music would be represented by Mantovani or "Friday Night Is Music Night" on BBC Radio Two. It turned out that the concert was given by a group of quite brilliant Russian music students from Moscow. Russia, in Communist days, set great store on obtaining successes in the big international music competitions, and these young stars had been sent on a tour down the Adriatic coastline to perfect their repertoire by performing nightly to any audience to be found – no question of fees. On this particular evening, the programme was way above the previous musical experience of the vast majority of the audience. I remember it started with a young girl of about fourteen who gave a startlingly brilliant performance of the Liszt Piano Sonata in B minor, then an eighteen year old violinist completely mystified his listeners with an impeccable rendering of the vast C major Fugue for solo violin by Bach, following this with one of the six unaccompanied sonatas by Ysaye – fiendishly difficult and very specialized to say the least. So it went on. A cellist played the solo Kodaly sonata, and I seem to remember they finished with Beethoven's "Archduke" Piano Trio. Not by any means seaside holiday fare. To their credit, the audience listened attentively in a rather bemused way. Nobody could fail to be impressed with the expertise and dedication of the young virtuosos, though the applause was generally rather lukewarm, which was such a shame – they deserved a standing ovation.

Further Scrapings

On the way out one heard remarks like "Well, it was quite nice, reely" Muriel and I went round the back to meet the young players, and in spite of the language barrier, managed to express a little of our appreciation, which seemed to please them.

The point I want to make is that the Communist totalitarian state, having identified musicians of talent, would give them everything necessary for their training, including the final polish of real performing experience, their one and only aim in life being to perform the virtuoso repertoire on their particular instruments to the highest possible level. It was a perfect way to produce youngsters who would play amazingly in the big competitions, but the training was very one-sided. David Oistrakh, an artist of the very highest standard, regardless of his country of origin, is reported to have expressed to a friend of mine his disapproval of this concentration of effort to produce prize winners by more or less force feeding youngsters from the earliest age. To paraphrase his words, he said – "They work and slave away to play their Paganini Caprices and all the great concertos, then from age eighteen to twenty-five they do the rounds of all the competitions, winning prizes to the greater glory of Communism. Then they suddenly become too old to enter the competitions. They have no experience of ensemble playing, chamber music or orchestral, their sight reading is poor, and they find they can't even get a job at the back of the second violins in the Kiev Opera House!"

We in the West have to struggle harder to get our training and experience. Perhaps that made things harder for us, but in some ways it might be considered a healthier situation. We may produce fewer violinists who can perform all the Paganini 24 Caprices from memory, but I reckon that we do train a greater number of excellent musicians who can fit into the body of musical performance – who are, so-to-speak the highly accomplished "middle class" of the musical world, useful in orchestras, chamber groups, occasionally as soloists, with a wide knowledge of the repertoire, and able to lead an interesting and varied musical life. The few who are destined for world stardom will inevitably rise through the ranks through sheer force of personality. But remember, it takes artistry and talent to play the second violin part of a Haydn symphony, and a violinist who does nothing but practice the Brahms concerto can be pretty useless in an orchestral string section.

Chapter 14 – Scraping a Living – The Freelance Scene

I have already written quite a bit about the freelance work available in post-war London, but a few more reminiscences remain to be told.

Firstly, I must point out an error in my previous book; Scraping a Living.

On pages 124-125 I refer to the cellist Jack Alexander, and my great cellist friend Dennis Vigay has pointed out to me that the name was <u>Fred</u> Alexander. My memory had gone astray, and I was confusing him with Jack Alexandra, a well-known bassoonist at that time.

Readers may remember that I recalled playing incidental music at the Apollo Theatre, Shaftsbury Avenue with Fred and the pianist Teddy Krish for the comedy play *"Seagulls over Sorrento"* starring Ronald Shiner. Those evenings were always great fun. Teddy Krish, although he seemed rather a dry character, had a nice sardonic sense of humour, and was an excellent player, both in classical and jazz music. He took great pleasure in arranging Bach Choral Preludes for the piano and had several of them published. As I have noted before he was inordinately proud of the fact that Myra Hess often played one of his arrangements as an encore.

Fred Alexander was one of those people with a true streak of genius, but who never rose to the heights of which he was really capable. Every cellist in London would say "Oh, old Freddie really is a fantastic player!" but that was as far as it went. He would be welcome in any orchestra or light music ensemble, but never aspired to anything greater. He did broadcasts of piano trios with the violinist Oscar Lampe, another exceptional technical genius, but they were never really successful. Probably Fred was basically a bit lazy. He loved the company of fellow players, he probably preferred light music, as long as it was good, and I don't blame him for that. He was a character who stands out boldly in the memory, and I am grateful to have known him and played with him.

It was quite amazing how that show ran on for such a long spell at the Apollo. There were full houses at practically every performance – twice on Saturday, which could become a bit tedious. Sometimes from the pit we could get glimpses of the audience, and all sorts of famous faces appeared in the front of the stalls. One night I looked up and saw a face that seemed terribly familiar, though strange to see it laughing. It was, incredibly Boris Karloff, star of many Hollywood horror films!

Inevitably, on a long run like that, crises occur and things go wrong. The play was a sort of comedy thriller and the action takes place exclusively on the mess-deck of a secret naval establishment – location unknown – with an all male cast. The story details I don't remember, but in the last act Bernard Lee, who took the part of second in command to Ronald Shiner's Chief Petty Officer, was sent off on some vital secret mission. Tension builds up, and at the climax of the whole thing there is a terrific explosion off-stage. Consternation! Everyone thinks their pals have all been killed – but it all works out alright in the end.

On one particular Saturday night, I decided to stay in the pit and watch the show (we were only required to play in the intervals.) The first act was going smoothly on its way, with cheerful banter between the various characters, when someone by mistake triggered off the last act's explosion. The great unexpected bang shook the audience out of their seats, but the actors, with incredible professional aplomb ignored it completely and with only the slightest hiatus continued the show. But behind scenes there was panic. They didn't have any more explosive or whatever was needed for the bang, and it being Saturday there was no way of getting some more from whoever was the supplier. So, when it came to the last act, at the required moment there was a sound from off-stage rather like somebody bursting a paper bag, and Shiner and company had to react as if an atom bomb had gone off!

Another supreme cock-up I remember was later in the run. Bernard Lee, who was an equally well-known star as Shiner, left the cast in order to film an American version of the show at Elstree studios. The day came when they finished the filming, and apparently there was a riotous party in the studio to celebrate. After much heavy drinking, Bernard Lee took a taxi down to the West End, turned up at the Apollo Theatre, and being completely out of his mind, had the mad idea of going on after the explosion and doing the last bit of the play himself for old times sake, regardless of the fact that he was dressed in American seaman's uniform, and the play was about the British Navy. They had to restrain him forcibly. At one point he even burst into the pit where we were playing the few little bits of music required during the last act. Everything was chaos – we didn't get our proper queues, and I don't know what the audience thought!

There was one very rare occasion when all three of us were off on other engagements, and we had three deps (deputies) in. It was our general practice to go out for coffee during the longer breaks, and we all knew to the second when we should be back. But on this occasion, the trio went out wrongly in the third act, and after a leisurely cup of coffee and a chat, came back to find the whole theatre locked up and the lights out! They should have been there to play the National Anthem and some cheerful music to see the audience out. Not only that, their instruments were left exposed in the pit. What a fiasco!

The show deserved its success, because it was very entertaining, thoroughly professional, and had a great cast. Bernard Lee as the second lead will be remembered in many films of that time – a real tough-guy character. Ronald Shiner, the star, for some reason is not as well known today. He was a great quick-talking cockney comedian, and I always admired him for the way he always gave absolutely 100% to every performance – never any let-up. His most striking characteristic was an enormously large bulbous red nose; rumour had it that he had insured it at Lloyds of London for six thousand dollars!

My main jobs at this time were in the Boyd Neel String Orchestra from 1947 to 1951, and then with the Philharmonia until 1955. I have written pretty extensively about these orchestras in my previous book, so I will only say here that I have always remained sincerely grateful to them both for giving me whatever expertise in ensemble playing I have been able to use in my work ever since. I think I have been lucky enough to be with them for what was in many ways their golden days. Certainly I can remember hosts of great concerts, with some of the greatest conductors and soloists of the century.

However, both were free-lance orchestras, unlike those of the BBC whose players worked on a regular salary, so sometimes we were comfortably off financially and other times we were struggling. Important, therefore, to be on good terms with the "fixers" who would ring up for deputies for the other orchestras like the RPO, the LSO, and the other chamber orchestras such as the Jacques, and various other entirely free-lance bands. In the latter category there was one I played for quite regularly; that was the Vic Oliver Concert Orchestra.

Vic Oliver was a well-known comedian who starred with Bebe Daniels and Ben Lyon in the popular BBC programme "Hi Gang" He was the first castaway on Desert Island Discs. He was a skilled musician and played the violin (badly for a joke in his shows). He was born in Vienna where he had early musical training. He had aspirations as a conductor and founded his own eponymous Concert Orchestra which gave light classical concerts along the South coast.[15]

Through my theatre work in the West End, I got to know an elderly fiddle player called Vic Allchurch who was the fixer for Vic Oliver, and he began booking me for Vic Oliver dates, which were mostly seaside Sunday night events. I started at the back of the 1st violins, but on the second date I had a meteoric rise. The programme included Wagner Tannhauser Overture, which includes one section of solos for the front desk players. The leader has a relatively easy part, playing a soaring Wagnerian leitmotif. The number two however, has a much more demanding *obligato* with quite difficult arpeggios ranging through various keys. On this particular day the regular number two player was away, and the next man in line took one look at this passage and said "I'm not playing that!" Most of the others were rather elderly fiddlers who did nothing but rank-and-file playing and would never stick their necks out in front of the section. So I, in the brashness of youth shouted out from the back "I'll do it". It went alright, so ever after I was Vic Oliver's sub principal.

Further Scrapings

Vic was not by any means a good conductor, but his fame meant that we always got full houses. At rehearsals, there was never any sign of the comedian's patter and jollity. Far from it – he took the whole thing very seriously and was quite a martinet in demanding attention and efficiency, even if he was not all that efficient himself.

He was always strict about not wasting time and beginning promptly. There was one rather macabre incident in Eastbourne. The orchestra was shambling on to the stage after their long trip down from London, and Vic was already on the podium exhorting them to get settled down. "Come on, come on please – we've a lot to get through" and so on and so on. One very elderly viola player was slowly making his way to the back of the section, when there was an awful disturbance, and he fell over in a confusion of chairs and instruments. My friend, cellist Jack Holmes was sub-principal of the Philharmonia and he was then leading the cellos for Vic. He quickly put his instrument down, rushed across, and felt for the old chap's heart beat.

Vic was meanwhile continuing to try to get things going – "Come on – come on please, get settled down. What's the matter there? We're wasting time!"

"But Vic" said Jack – "We can't, we can't. He's - he's dead!"

"Oh, surely not" came the reply. How thoughtless to die in my rehearsal! It was of course tragic, but one felt that the old boy himself as a typical orchestral player would have appreciated the irony of the conductor's attitude.

It reminds me of the story about Ted Heath, the dance band leader, who just as the band was setting off on tour was told that his principal trumpet had died. "My God" he said – "Everything happens to me".

These kind of dates were fine to help keep body and soul together, but it was important to try at the same time to build up a reputation and do more serious work.

When I came out of the Marines in 1947, I was still having lessons with Fred Grinke, who was leader of the Boyd Neel and someone

I admired greatly, both as a violinist and as a person. He was an absolutely straightforward character and someone that you felt you could trust – more like a friend than a teacher, though his actual teaching was first-rate. He was a great help to me, and when Muriel and I told him we wanted to do an audition for the BBC, he gave us very good advice. This was: make sure that whatever you play, you are confident that you can play it well; above all that you really love it as music, and never play something that will stretch you unduly, just because you think it will impress the panel.

We followed his advice – preparing items by Vivaldi, Beethoven, Schumann and finishing with Bartok Roumanian Dances – all music that we loved and had played many times in public. On the way into the audition at the BBC Maida Vale studios we bumped into our old friend from wartime days, John Kirkland, the talented fellow inhabitant of our student digs in Marlborough Place. John was already established as a member of the BBC Unit which provided regular light music every day of the week. He said to me "Hello, Peter, what are you doing in here?" I told him I was doing an audition to get some solo work. John looked at me quizzically, nodded his head and said - "Hmm... Yeah... You'll be alright!" Maybe because of his natural ability and also his naivety you could somehow trust John's instinct and I went into that audition feeling I had been given a boost.

Those kinds of occasions were pretty terrifying. You're in an empty studio. A curtain is drawn over the glass window into the balance box, and you just have to start playing when the green light comes on. You've no idea who your listeners are – you imagine they are all laughing and joking, and probably having a cup of tea. It's up to you to pour your heart out and give your best to the bare cream coloured studio walls, with nothing to comfort you but the distant hum of the central heating. Afterwards, a studio attendant comes in, thanks you very much, shakes your hand and tells you to expect a letter in about a fortnight. You go home feeling absolutely deflated!

The letter did come, and it was good news. Muriel and I began to get pretty regular engagements for studio recitals that continued more

Further Scrapings

or less throughout our careers. In those days, young up-and-coming artists were offered morning mini-recitals of about 45 minutes between 9 and 10 am. They were absolutely live – no recordings then, and if there were any slips it was just too bad! Nowadays we live in the age of retakes available in case of accident, but then you lived dangerously. You got up about 6 am, drove to the studios for a 7.30 balance test, had a nervous cup of coffee in the canteen, a quick warm up, then start the performance, trying to make yourself feel that you are in front of a lovely audience and it is 7.30 in the evening, when all concerts should be!

Looking back, we did quite a lot of interesting programmes, and we were also often asked to broadcast specific works that we had to learn specially. Stravinsky, Hindemith, Martinu, many others were broadcast over the years. It was also good to get to know the various BBC producers of the music programmes. One who specially springs to mind was Robert Simpson, composer of a number of fine symphonies, and we played some of his violin and piano compositions.

Muriel was also doing regular broadcasts with the Judy Hill Trio. I was fortunate enough to catch the attention of Rae Jenkins, then the conductor of the BBC Welsh Orchestra, and he invited me to play concertos regularly with him in Cardiff. Rae was an extraordinary character. He had been a near neighbour of ours in King Henry's Road. Before the War he had been the viola player in light music ensembles led by Campoli, and it was only after the War that he branched out as a conductor. I played a wide variety of lesser-known repertoire with him. One remarkable piece which Rae asked me to learn and play with the orchestra was the Pibroch Suite by Sir Alexander Mackenzie. Rae knew of it because Mackenzie was Principal of the Royal Academy of Music between 1888 and 1924, and Rae was a student there in 1922. Mackenzie had been a close friend of the great Spanish violinist Pablo de Sarasate, who commissioned this fine work for the Leeds Festival in 1889, where he gave the first performance conducted by the composer.

It is contemporary with and also very similar to the Scottish Fantasy by Max Bruch, a piece well known to most violinists. For some reason the music of Mackenzie has been for many years almost completely neglected, and it is due to the interest of the Hyperion Gramophone Company that he is now hailed as a significant Late Romantic composer, having written music that is beautiful to hear and highly accomplished.

I also began to get engagements to play chamber music, both concerts and broadcasts. Quite a lot of this was with the London Harpsichord Ensemble, the creation of the flautist John Francis with his wife, Millicent Silver; I have written about this in my previous book. I was also leading some other ad hoc ensembles, but my main ambition still escaped me, which was to lead a symphony orchestra. My chance came in 1955 when John Pritchard invited me to travel North with him and take up the post of leader of the Liverpool Philharmonic Orchestra.

Chapter 15 – Money Matters

Before I move on to the next stage of the story, which covers our stay in Liverpool, I want to say a few words about money – the wages and fees that we musicians earn, and how this has changed over the years of my career, but in other ways how it is really basically the same.

There is a view held by some members of the general public that we musicians are above all such mundane things as financial considerations. We play our instruments by some wondrous talent that we had from birth. No work or training is really needed – it just comes naturally to us. We do it because we love it, so whether we are paid or not is a matter of complete indifference to us. In any case, what we are doing is not real work – we are just doing it to enjoy ourselves. Obviously we only have to do a couple of hours of so-called work in the evening at a concert. The rest of the time we just laze about and live on our private means, which are probably extensive, or perhaps we have another proper job – maybe as a bank manager or possibly a road sweeper!

Others think that because we may occasionally appear on television or broadcast on the BBC we enjoy vast fees which enable us to live a life of luxury. Because we have the good fortune to be talented, we are able to escape the hard labour to earn a living which is the lot of most poor mortals. So we are the object of envy, rather than admiration – lucky so-and-sos, just doing what they like doing, and actually getting paid for it!

One nice anecdote illustrates this attitude. My son, Paul, who is also a violinist, remembers having a phone call from a friend of his, a very successful architect, who was also a keen amateur musician and conducted an amateur choir. The conversation went as follows.

"O hello Paul, I wonder if you could help me out. Our choir is putting on a performance of "The Messiah" on Christmas Eve – complete with orchestra, and I wondered if you could come along and lead the orchestra for us?"

"Oh well, I don't know – on Christmas Eve? I was hoping to be at home. Well, can you tell me – what's the fee?"

"O no – there's no fee. We're all amateurs you know, and we're just doing it for fun."

"Aha, aha, I see – no fee, just doing it for fun. Very good. Well, to change the subject slightly – I'm thinking of having an extension built to my house. It will be a pretty big job. D'you think you could survey it, draw up the plans and get planning permission for me; oversee the whole project – just for fun you know?"

"Ahem, ah well – yes" somewhat abashed – "I see what you mean!"

The truth of course is, that professional musicians endeavour to get and expect to achieve an income and standard of living comparable to any other skilled occupation, requiring ability and training. They very reasonably expect to be paid for what they do, at a rate similar to everybody else. Obviously they vary in terms of success, and I am pretty sure that on average they do not attain the same financial level as do doctors, lawyers, civil servants and similar professionals. But, on the whole, they mostly lead comfortable lives and achieve a reasonable standard of living. Most of them have the great advantage that they are doing something that they want to do, and whatever the occupation may be that you choose; if you truly love it you have the chance of a life free from frustration.

Throughout many years of teaching the violin, I have not often recommended my pupils to take up music professionally. I know that there are many easier ways of earning a comfortable living. But, if you have the natural ability and you sincerely love music, then you will make it in the end and have every chance of leading a life of fulfillment.

I am not going to quote many actual figures to show different payments from the past up to the present, as inflation has made such comparisons meaningless. I remember as a boy before the War, being told by my father, who was quite financially conscious, that he was proud of the fact that his fairly recently established music teaching connection was now generally bringing in about £20 a week from the combined work of himself and my mother. This was the time when mill workers would expect to earn not much more than £3 a week. Another more recent milestone in the inflationary spiral I vividly remember. It was in 1981 when we were living in Glasgow. Our great friend, the conductor Meredith Davies was working with Scottish Opera for a week and staying at our house. One evening he took us and a couple of friends out to dinner at the Grosvenor Hotel. We went into the bar before the meal, and Meredith ordered a round of drinks for us all. He came back from paying for it, saying ruefully – "Look, this idea of going out for a meal is getting beyond a joke. I've just bought these few drinks for us, and can you believe it, I've got very little change out of a pound!"

So, actual figures are wildly different, but the proportion between costs and earnings stays more or less the same. However, there are some marked differences in the rates for the job as it were. When I was first doing work as a soloist and chamber music player for the BBC, it was quite obvious that the Corporation was taking advantage of the fact that young aspiring musicians were desperately keen to get their name known, and would have broadcast for nothing if asked. For one of those early morning recitals, for which we would have rehearsed and worked for weeks, I remember we were paid £15 between us, which was pretty despicable even in those days. I remember concerto dates with the BBC Welsh and occasionally the BBC Midland Light Orchestra in Birmingham, getting £20. And to do those kinds of things, apart from the hours of practice involved, often meant turning down two or three recording sessions with the Philharmonia when I could have been sitting comfortably in the middle of the fiddle section with no nerve strain, and earning a lot more! No wonder some friends thought I was crazy, chasing around trying to get these dates. But I didn't regret it – it was worth making the effort to build some sort of an enhanced reputation, and above all there was the satisfaction of doing something really worthwhile, and the thrill of achievement.

In 1949 and 1950, Muriel and I made another big commitment to try to enhance our reputation. We had done a joint recital in the Duke's

Hall of the RAM just before I went into the Marines, but now we felt it was important to play together in a major London concert centre. So, like other young hopefuls of the day, we put on two recitals at the Wigmore Hall in London's West End. In those days, such ventures would generally get a half-column in either the Times or the Telegraph, and we were lucky enough to get notices which furnished enough favourable snippets to go in our publicity brochure. But of course, hire of hall, programmes, publicity and management fees were nowhere nearly covered by ticket sales, so this was another example of the higher you aimed the less you earned. Still in the end it was well worth the sacrifice.

I remember one incident at our first recital there. In those days, there was a very elderly gentleman who was in some way attached to the Wigmore Hall as a sort of assistant or attendant, and who took it upon himself to act as the obligatory page-turner for all the pianists. Muriel was landed with him and immediately felt a strong distrust of his capabilities, which was only too soon justified. One of our items was the Duo Concertante by Stravinsky, the fourth movement of which is a Gigue, consisting of break-neck fast semiquaver triplets throughout with no gaps at all. She was absolutely depending on this elderly person for efficient help, so imagine her feeling when approaching the first page turn she glanced to the left and found to her consternation that he was sitting there, eyes closed, mouth open, snoring slightly and fast asleep!

As I have said earlier, some of my friends and colleagues saw clearer than I, that light music and session work was the best way to earn a decent living. I have done my share of that, but although good light music is fun to do, as a full-time occupation it can be pretty soul-destroying, so I don't regret the efforts we made, even though they were not always financially advantageous.

Orchestral playing is a minefield of different rates for different players. There are three main divisions – principal, sub-principal and rank-and-file. I hate that last term, rank-and-file, implying that you are the lowest of the low. Practically all wind players and percussionists are either principals or sub-principals, meaning they get about 20% or 10% above the basic rate, whilst nearly all the strings, apart from the

Further Scrapings

front desks are the dreaded rank-and-file – to be compared with what is known in the army as the PBI – poor bloody infantry. True, they don't have the responsibility of soloistic exposure, and if they miss out the odd note nobody notices. But they play far more actual notes than the wind. They generally have more difficult music to play. If a considerate conductor organizes his rehearsals so that people don't have to hang around waiting too much, it is invariably the strings who have to stay on to the very last – and very often the first fiddles who have to stay on even longer for special difficulties!

Nowadays a number of players in a string section may well be able to negotiate special rates. The ideal of any string section, of course, is that everyone, right to the back, is a potential leader, and you sometimes get that feeling when you see an orchestra like the Berlin Philharmonic on TV. The body-language of all the strings, right to the back, is of 100% effort – maybe because they are really glad to get this date, and there are a whole list of players who would like to have been asked instead of them. That is because the rate of pay for orchestral musicians in Germany, and also in the USA is considerably higher than in this country.

The orchestral leader is in a different category. Generally he (or she) can command double the basic rate, but this covers the considerable soloistic responsibilities, the responsibility of liaison between the conductor and orchestra, and the technical advice and help to the entire string section.

Individual wind principals may well be able to command special rates. I have no inside information as to these details, but I am pretty sure that Dennis Brain, the phenomenal horn player in the Philharmonia, got at least the same fee as the leader, Manoug Parikian. But maybe he didn't. To get what you are worth, you need a hard-headed agent. When I was young, footballers got £20 a week during the season if they were lucky. Now, aided by agents and supplemented by advertising contracts, they regularly are paid more than the Prime Minister!

Peter Mountain

People have commented on the growing preponderance of women players, especially in the strings of present day orchestras. It is undoubtably true that many women are equally, perhaps even more talented than men in musical performance, and may well show superior application as students. But, I think that the real reason is financial. The basic salary offered by most British orchestras is ample for a single girl, but for a man with a wife and family to support, it will mean living on the poverty line. That is why many musicians have partners who are also musicians, and who balance their careers between both doing professional work, and both sharing the domestic responsibilities of household and families.

So, to sum up my experiences up to 1955, the freelance world of London music gave me a wide-spread experience of most branches of the profession, and I felt quite well equipped to pass on to the next stage.

Chapter 16 – Leading

Before I go on to have a further look at Liverpool days, I would like to write a few words about the job which had been my ultimate ambition – leading a full symphony orchestra.

What does the orchestral leader actually do?

This is a question that I have often been asked, and I always feel that, in just a sentence or two, I have only been able to give a pretty unsatisfactory answer. So here is an attempt to define to some extent what the various facets of his or her job are.

I say his or her because it has been normal in the past to assume that the leader will be a man. In fact we are only just (in some cases) moving away from the time when all professional orchestral players were invariably male. Sir Thomas Beecham famously justified this when he said he would never have women in his orchestra because if they were pretty they would distract the men, and if they were ugly they would distract him! My great friend and colleague, Marie Wilson, was undoubtedly the finest woman orchestral player of her day, and was assured by Sir Adrian Boult that if only she were a man she would be the best leader of her time. The highest post she could obtain was to be sub-leader of the BBC Symphony Orchestra, sitting with Paul Beard, though she did regularly lead what was known as the Section C Orchestra, a smaller group used for some broadcasts. The Scottish Orchestra (now the Royal Scottish Symphony Orchestra) was led just after the war by an outstanding woman player Jean Rennie, but when Karl Rankl took over conductorship in 1951 he insisted that she was replaced by Thomas Matthews. When I was young I used to attend the Hallé concerts in Bradford, when Beecham was the regular conductor, the leader was Alfred Barker and not a single woman was to be seen. Women soloists were regularly present, but in the orchestra absolutely all were men. Now the situation is very different. The Hallé's first violin section is quite predominantly female, and is led with great distinction by Lynn Fletcher. Most orchestras include members selected entirely by ability, with no sexual discrimination whatsoever.

It may be that in the past, it was assumed that the post of leader needs a tougher outlook and personality than a woman should be asked to assume. Women soloists have long been admired on the concert platform. Mozart wrote his great B flat Violin Sonata K454 to be played by himself and a well-known violinist from Mantua, Regina Strinasacchi (1764-1839). Nearer to our time, the violinist Wilma Neruda (1838-1911) was married to Sir Charles Hallé in 1891 and as Lady Hallé became a famous soloist throughout Europe. Many other great women violinists over the years spring to mind. Yet, it is only in very recent years that the last bastions of male chauvinism regarding orchestral membership, such as the Vienna Philharmonic Orchestra, have been slowly and reluctantly breached!

So, what are the exact qualities required from a leader, that it is now accepted, can be shown by a violinist of either sex?

Obviously, he or she must have abilities as a player that command the respect of all the others, and are clearly obvious to the public. There may be players of great, even outstanding ability, whose qualities do not include the degrees of assertiveness and leadership that are needed to act as a fine edge to the string section as a whole. The ability to perform violin concertos is different from that needed for the great orchestral solos, such as we find in Strauss "Heldenleben", Rimsky Korsakov "Scheherazade", or the big ballet solos by Tchaikovsky. Once you are settled into a concerto performance the tension lessens somewhat, whereas the ability to cope with being suddenly exposed soloistically in the middle of a work requires quite a different kind of nerve, which some find less easy to cope with. The word "solo" printed above the briefest of passages can transform many a competent player into a gibbering wreck!

The leader must also be able to make firm and convincing decisions regarding matters of bowing and fingering. These things are often not obvious and can lead to endless debates, but the leader must avoid unnecessary time-wasting, and be able to say firmly "This is what we are going to do." He (or she) must also make sure the decisions are defensible and reasonably permanent, because nothing annoys orchestral players more than constant alterations of bowing!

A leader's responsibilities, however, go much further than this. I speak here not just of a leader of an ad-hoc ensemble created for one or two specific concerts, but a leader of an established orchestra, with continual, whole-time commitment to the performance of a continuous series of concerts in a specific environment, under the direction of an overall music director and conductor. In other words, the leadership of one of the large orchestras that are found in all the greatest cities of the world.

The person holding this post must have an empathy with the conductor based on mutual respect and similarity of musical outlook. Ideally, the conductor expresses his own conceptions and desires regarding the music to be played in general broad terms. These are translated by the leader into specific technical decisions, very often to do with bowing.

As regards bowing, there is much that needs clarification here.

Bowing is by no means just a question of ups and downs. From the audience it certainly looks good to see a whole string section absolutely synchronized in the bow strokes. This is true, despite the example of Leopold Stokovsky who insisted on free bowing in order to get a continuous seamless flow of tone quality. (No-one else, to my knowledge, has followed his example to any extent.) However, there are other things to consider. The speed of the bow is infinitely variable and must be similarly controlled by all players. Also, the placing of the bow on the string, either near the bridge or the fingerboard, is vitally important as it alters the type of sound produced. The part of the bow to be used - either the tip, the middle or the heel – all need careful consideration. A soloist, having only his own performance to consider, has relative freedom to vary these as the spirit moves him. However, in a string section, the ideal is to have the same kind of tone quality from all the players, so a considerable degree of rational thought must be shown in rehearsals, and the responsibility for this is ultimately taken by the leader.

There are some conductors, generally those who were originally string players, who have very definite ideas about the bowing they want. One of these was Sir John Barbirolli, who started his career as a very accomplished cellist. I never played for Barbirolli, though I knew him as a friend and had immense respect for him. I attended several of his rehearsals, and witnessed the way he demanded absolute attention to the bowing marks on his parts, which he had personally meticulously marked.

But, in spite of this example, I have always found it is best if the conductor indicates the general shape of the music, the kind of sound he wants, and leaves it to the players with their specialized knowledge to work out how to achieve it. Players like to feel they are making a contribution to the artistic result, rather than being just pawns in the game, blindly following orders.

This brings me to a particular anecdote about Barbirolli that I still remember vividly. In the early sixties when I was leading the Royal Liverpool Philharmonic Orchestra, we had several visits from Henryck Szeryng. On one occasion he came as soloist and conductor and I was asked to play the Bach Double Concerto with him. He was very friendly and gave me several lessons that were immensely valuable. His next engagement after Liverpool was to play the Brahms concerto with Barbirolli and the Hallé in the old Free Trade Hall, and he insisted that I should come over to Manchester with him. I sat in on the rehearsal and listened to the balance, and of course attended the concert and met Barbirolli afterwards.

It was a lovely occasion and I enjoyed it very much. However I was rather amused by one part of the concert. Barbirolli was a musician immersed in the classical and romantic era of big orchestral sound, wanting warm and generous playing. The Baroque era of music making was not his most natural environment, but on this occasion the concert began with a performance of Bach Brandenburg Concerto No.1. He prefaced this with a little speech to the audience, which as far as I can remember went roughly as follows:

"Ladies and Gentlemen: We are now going to play the beautiful Brandenburg Concerto by Bach. Now, I would like you to understand,

Further Scrapings

that this is not big orchestral music. It is really much more like true chamber music – the music of friends. This little group is around me this evening; we will just be making music between ourselves, in a truly intimate relationship.

So, I shall not stand in the middle as a conductor, but instead will sit on this seat, and quietly preside over their participation, as one musician amongst many!"

He then turned, sat down on his little seat, with a humble and quiet demeanour. But, as soon as the music began, he used his normal long baton with all the immense, sweeping gestures and tremendous authority he would exercise in conducting an Elgar Symphony!

It made me realize the truth; that conductors and soloists have their own individual ideas and beliefs, and they generally will not deviate from them. In fact, the greatest have to be absolutely committed to their personal views of the music. Kreisler said that he never taught, because he could not tolerate anything that was different from his own conception. They may, to some extent, vary them from performances of one composer to another, but they only have their own ideas to consider. We, as orchestral players, must change our playing of say a Beethoven Symphony to suit various conductors at the drop of a hat. Different ideas may (or may not!) be equally valid, but it requires tremendous flexibility from the players to accommodate these changes. This is part of our job as orchestral members.

An orchestra generally has a chief conductor, and during his term of office he will impose some of his principal ideas on the playing style of the orchestra. As I have said, he needs a leader who is sympathetic to those ideas, and who often will be called upon to translate them into practicalities. Barbirolli had Laurence Turner as a leader when he first was in Manchester, but soon after came his successor, Martin Milner, with whom he had a most productive collaboration. I was lucky in my eleven years in Liverpool to work with two main conductors, John Pritchard and Charles Groves. They were very different personalities and musicians, but I respected them, and they both became my very good friends. Examples of this kind of working together go back through the years. There exists an interesting engraving of the first violin section of the Leipzig Gewandhaus Orchestra when Mendelssohn conducted it. The leader was Ferdinand David, dedicatee of Mendelssohn's concerto, and it is interesting to note that all the violins play standing up. All are absolutely equal, except for David, who stood on a little box!

Actually, I do think that it is important for the players to be able to see the leader as well as the conductor, so that they can feel the influence of the general style of playing. However, it is important to realize here the importance of peripheral vision. In an orchestra, you don't need to look directly at the leader, or even at the conductor. The beat and the bowing can be seen, as we say, out of the corner of the eye. Here is a description from the Internet of this phenomenon:

> *Peripheral vision is a part of* vision *that occurs outside the very centre of gaze. There are two types of receptor cells,* rod cells *and* cone cells; *rod cells are unable to distinguish color and are predominant at the periphery, while cone cells are concentrated mostly in the center of the retina (the* macula).
>
> *Peripheral vision is good at detecting motion (a feature of rod cells), and is relatively strong at night or in the dark, when the lack of color cues and lighting makes cone cells far less useful. This makes it useful for avoiding predators, who tend to hunt at night and may attack unexpectedly.*
>
> From Wikipedia, the free encyclopedia.

I specially like the last sentence. The human ability to guard against predators is equally useful against conductors, who also hunt at night and may attack unexpectedly!

There are some conductors who constantly want people to watch the beat. They are generally of the megalomaniac type. Marie Wilson very wisely said – "I never look at the beat – I look at their eyes! Then you know whether they've got anything to give!" You can see the movement of the baton, which in a good conductor describes the shape of the music – not just the beat. Any decent player can keep time. Otto Klemperer used to roar at us "You might at least play together!" In other words – that's your responsibility.

There are some conductors who bombard the players with vague ideas, but have no real conception of what they actually want, and certainly no idea of how to get it. One such I encountered recently was constantly asking the violins for more warmth. Every player tries to please him by either using more vibrato, though there is a limit as to what is possible here, or maybe more bow, or simply rolling about a bit in the seat. (This often satisfies this type of individual.) Also, if they can just see more hectic left hand activity, they feel they have done something. But the trouble is that everyone is trying in different ways and often there is no real change in the tone – it just averages out. The leader's job here is clear. It is no good trying to have a confrontation with the maestro by asking him what he means by warmth or how he expects us to achieve it, because he simply doesn't know. Instead, just take over for a minute; turn to the section and say "Listen chaps, I think what we need is a bit less bow, a bit nearer the bridge, and a slightly quicker vibrato – not too much!" or words to that effect. If everyone does this, there will certainly be an audible difference, and it is most likely that the response will be "Yeah, yeah, that's beautiful. Thank-you!" Or if it is - "No – no; that's not what I want at all!" – at least you know he has got a pair of ears, and you can try asking for away from the bridge with a light *flautando* bow stroke, or whatever is appropriate. But, whatever you do, don't lecture the players or even lecture the conductor! We are all in it together, trying to find solutions.

Sometimes, even great composers can be mistaken in the way they mark the score to achieve the effect they have in mind. In 1960, the Liverpool orchestra commissioned from Sir William Walton his Second Symphony, and the world premier was given at the Edinburgh Festival on 2 September, conducted by our music director, Sir John Pritchard. However, there was a previous performance in Liverpool conducted by Walton, so we were privileged to do the very first rehearsals on it with the composer himself.

I remember the first morning rehearsal session vividly. The first violins start the work with an entry on the last beat of the third bar with a typical Walton phrase; a C sharp and D in quavers, swooping up in the next bar to a high C sharp dotted crotchet, then subsiding to quaver B flat and falling back to the original D. This is a remarkable arch-like figure upon which the whole movement is built. Walton had written a crescendo up to the top note that was marked with an accent, which seemed logical and appropriate, but when we played it first he immediately said – "Please, not too much crescendo". We rehearsed it again, and he obviously couldn't get us to play it as he wished. We went on to rehearse the rest of the movement, and at the interval he was still dissatisfied with our opening. He spoke to me in the Green Room, saying we were still overdoing the crescendo. I said – "Could we try a diminuendo?" "No, no" he said –"I don't want that." "Well, can I just try something else?" We went back for the second half, and I said to the section "Instead of starting the up beat with an up bow, which seems natural, let's begin with a down bow, then we arrive at an up bow for the peak of the phrase, the top D, making almost a *subito* piano but with extra expressive vibrato." We played it, and he immediately said "Yes, yes; that's perfect!" It produced a sort of sudden catch of breath – a kind of diminuendo producing an emotional crescendo!

I am pleased to say that my bowing is now printed in the published score, with an expressive line instead of an accent on the top note and no crescendo. It's the kind of phrase colouring that you often hear on Heifetz records, and Heifetz of course was the dedicatee of Walton's violin concerto and a great friend of his.

As players, it is our job to listen carefully to every aspect of a performance, and try to analyze the exact technical means needed to produce a certain effect. Mere reliance on emotional reactions is never enough. Specific actions must be taken, and the leader of a string section must try to ensure either by example or instruction that everyone else is doing the same thing.

The other important function of the leader (and this relates to the whole orchestra, not just the strings) is to act as an intermediary between the players on one side and the conductor or the management on the other. Grievances and misunderstandings can spring up on either side, and if left to fester can become blown up out of all

Further Scrapings

proportions. The leader must see these things coming, and if possible find a diplomatic solution, often by a quiet word here and there. But above all, it must be seen and felt very clearly that the ultimate loyalty of the leader is to the orchestra, even if (as sometimes can happen) an orchestral colleague behaves unreasonably. He must get things out in the open and appeal to everyone's general good sense. Relationships in the closed atmosphere of orchestral life can easily become a little fraught, and a sympathetic word here and there is often all that is needed to relieve tension.

It is reassuring to the players when the leader is seen to respond promptly to any less than reasonable behavior by the conductor, such as exceeding rehearsal times. I have absolutely no sympathy with directors who want to carry on after the session should end, and then imply that the players ought to be censured for not wanting to give more time to ensure perfection. My very clear view is that if a conductor cannot do the job within the allotted time, he is incompetent. In fairness, also, the leader must be ready to censure lateness or inattention in the players.

So, there are a multitude of considerations that need thinking over, both on the platform and off. Within the section it is important to think about the seating of the players. Who gets on well with whom? Who are the people you would never put on the same desk! All these things need thinking about.

I asked a very experienced and fine player, what should be the qualities of a leader. Back came the immediate reply – "Someone who makes us feel good!"

I think that says it all!

Chapter 17 – Some Past Notable Orchestral Leaders

The first orchestral leader I had chance to observe was when as a schoolboy before the War I went to the Hallé Subscription Concerts in Bradford when the orchestra was led by Alfred Barker. Also, at that time, the second violins were led by a very young Leonard Hirsch, who went on to lead many other orchestras, including the Philharmonia, and with whom I was associated much later in chamber music and with the BBC Training Orchestra.

Alfred Barker (whom of course I never met but only observed from afar) seemed an enigmatic and fascinating character. In appearance he was medium height, lean, quick moving, and with a rather lantern-jawed visage, lined with the wide experiences of a varied life. I don't know much about his previous career, apart from the fact that he had spent time in pre-revolutionary Russia as a Court violinist in St. Petersburg. He certainly was a player to be reckoned with – his technique had bravura and flair, and it is worth while hunting out old records of the pre-war Hallé when he was on the front desk. The playing may not be of the overall perfection we are accustomed to today, but for sheer excitement and verve, especially when conducted by Hamilton Harty, it very often surpasses our modern efforts. Alfred Barker eventually left to become leader of the BBC Theatre Orchestra.

Albert Sammons (1886-1958) is now remembered as one of the greatest British soloists of all time. However, he worked up to his ultimate eminence by hard graft from relatively humble beginnings as a London fiddler who was virtually self-taught. In 1908, Sir Thomas Beecham was in the process of founding the Beecham Symphony Orchestra (BSO), recruiting the very finest young players around. The average age was 25. All was complete but he did not yet have a leader to satisfy him. However,

he was told of a highly promising young violinist in the salon orchestra at the Waldorf Hotel. Beecham went along and over dinner requested he play the last movement of the Mendelssohn's Violin Concerto, which the soloist took, as Beecham recalls, "at a speed which made me hold my breath". After dinner, when he had suggested to the young man that he play it again rather more slowly, the two men met. Albert Sammons was at once recruited into the BSO, as sub-leader to Philip Cathie for the first few months, and then as leader. He stayed for five years. According to Beecham, "he united a technical facility equal to any demand made upon it, a full, warm tone, a faultless rhythmic sense, and a brain that remained cool in the face of any untoward happening". Such was "the best all-round concertmaster" that Beecham had ever worked with.[16]

I never actually met Sammons, though I heard him in recitals and concertos, always with the greatest admiration, and also I played in the orchestra when he performed the Brahms concerto. It is a great regret not to have known this wonderful violinist personally, but I am very proud of the fact that Hugh Bean, who was then a colleague of mine in the Philharmonia and was a pupil of Sammons, told me that Albert had listened to one of my BBC recitals, and told him that the playing showed great promise. My friend, cellist Ambrose Gauntlett, who had been the first principal cello of the BBC and with whom I played much chamber music, told me that looking back over his lengthy career, the finest conductor he had worked for was Hamilton Harty, and the greatest leader by far was Albert Sammons.

A fine English violinist, whose basic achievements were as orchestral leader and chamber musician rather than as soloist, was George Stratton, born in London on 18 July 1897 who led the LSO from 1933 to 1953 and also the Glyndebourne Festival Orchestra from its inception in 1934. The Stratton String Quartet which he formed in 1925 (it lasted until 1942) gave many fine performances and its recording of the Elgar Piano Quintet with Harriet Cohen made in 1933, has passed into legend. In 1935 he published with Alan Frank, a book on The Playing of Chamber Music. He also contributed an article "On Leading the LSO" to Hubert Foss' *London Symphony*. He taught at the RCM from 1942 and was awarded an OBE in 1953. As a student I saw Stratton leading the LSO at several Prom concerts and was very impressed by his presence and personality at the head of the band. He made one realize that the body language of a leader is vitally important. I also remember fine Beethoven quartet performances by his group at the Wigmore Hall.

Arthur Catterall I have mentioned earlier as teacher of my student-days friend. John Kirkland. He was leader of the Hallé, but that was in the twenties, before my time. In 1930 he became the first leader of the BBC Symphony Orchestra, a post he held until 1936 when Paul Beard took over.

Catterall had in some ways a career similar to that of Albert Sammons as he concentrated more on a soloist's career. I met him quite often as a student, played in the chamber orchestra he conducted, and heard him as a soloist, notably in the concerto by E. J. Moeran, which was brilliant. Unfortunately he left very little recorded legacy, but I do have a CD copy of some short salon items which reveal playing of great character with an almost Heifetz type brilliance.

David McCallum (1897-1972) was an outstanding violinist born in Kilsyth. He learned locally from the age of seven and then at music academy in Glasgow. After winning a scholarship to the Royal College, London, at 14 he studied under Maurice Sons, a pupil of Wieniawski and leader of the Queens Hall Orchestra and came to model his playing on that of Fritz Kreisler.

Between 1932 and 1936 he led the Scottish Orchestra in Glasgow under Sir John Barbirolli, and then was asked by Sir Thomas Beecham to lead the London Philharmonic Orchestra. He led several top orchestras under conductors like Beecham, Bush, Klemperer, Sargent, and Toscanini but he also worked extensively as a freelance and on radio and television. By 1952 McCallum led the London Symphony Orchestra and he joined Mantovani in 1961 as leader of his orchestra on its international tours.

He was the father of the well known actor David McCallum Jnr, which led to the well-known quip when he was introduced to play a solo in a BBC show – "We can afford the father, but we can't afford the son!"

Further Scrapings

I knew David quite well, and had the privilege of sitting with him on several occasions as sub-leader. One of these was when the young David was still a schoolboy at University College, Hampstead, and the School was putting on a performance of St. John Passion by Bach. David senior was persuaded to lead the orchestra, and I was delighted to sit with him. As a player, he had a most gorgeous tone quality, and Kreisler is said to have admired him greatly. I remember he had a dislike of putting in too many marks in the parts. "No, no boy, leave it as it is. We'll remember, and we'll be free to play it by ear when the time comes." There was never any doubt that the playing of a section led by McCallum would produce a high quality sound. No wonder he was a great favourite of Mantovani, who specialized in a soaring, lush string section.

He was also notorious for the allegedly Scottish characteristic of being particularly tight in money matters, and many were the stories that went round the profession about this. He also did quite a bit of wheeling and dealing in buying and selling instruments; often purchasing violins from the main London dealers and selling them on at inflated prices which he could generally get quite easily when he himself demonstrated the wonderful tone they could produce. This came to a head at one time, when Hills of Bond Street, the world-leading violin experts, were supposed to have banned him from their shop! Still, he was a wonderful player, great company, and admired as a leader by everyone.

McCallum was never unkind in his judgments of fellow musicians, and he is reputed to have once said – "Ah, Paul Beard, now there's a real leader!", and in that he echoed the opinion of very many musicians.

Paul Beard, who led the BBC Symphony Orchestra from 1936 until his retirement in 1962, was maybe not the very finest violinist in London at the time, but there was certainly no other player who filled the post of leader with more efficiency, character and conviction.

His early background was leading the Spa Orchestra in Bridlington, and similar engagements in the North. In 1932, Beecham brought him to London to lead the newly-formed London Philharmonic, which he did for four years, alternating with David McCallum. But it was his time in the BBC which marked his greatest impact on British orchestral string playing. His knowledge of the repertoire was encyclopedic, and his playing provided an ideal clarity and definition to the string sound of a section. The orchestral solos were projected with character and suitable strength, musical and shapely but never drowned out by the orchestral texture, as I am afraid is only too often the case today. All wind and brass solos invariably come through to the audience with ease, but far too often string solos strive unsuccessfully to be heard. I wish some present day leaders would listen and learn from old BBC recordings with Paul leading. It was at a Prom in the Albert Hall that I remember particularly a performance of Vaughan Williams Serenade to Music – the orchestral version - which has extensive solo violin content. I have never heard it played with more conviction – not a trace of mere sentimentality, but real soaring cantabile which filled the entire hall and moved the spirit.

Paul was a tough character who would stand no nonsense from anyone. If he admired a conductor or a soloist, there was nothing he would not do to give support and help, but if he detected incompetence, or worse still pretention and insincerity, then woe betide. When you saw Paul leaning back in his chair, with an expression of complete exasperation on his rugged features, you should watch out for trouble!

My teacher at the RAM, Rowsby Woof, had taught Paul Beard in his youth, and from what we young players gathered, the pair of them had pretty much of a love-hate relationship. Rowsby used to tell us – "Paul was a fine player, but I could never get his bowing right. He had too much a mind of his own. I once threw the coal scuttle at him!" We didn't know whether to believe this or not. Paul's likes and dislikes grew more and more marked towards the end of his career; so much so that there were a growing number of conductors, some of international renown, who would not accept an engagement with the BBC if he was leading. He was no respecter of reputations. My dear friend and colleague, Tom Rowlette, who was Deputy Leader with me in Liverpool, had a spell in the BBC Symphony before coming to Liverpool, and Paul took quite a fancy to him, often having Tom come and sit up with him on the front desk. He used to tell Tom stories about playing with Richard Strauss conducting his own Tone Poems. He said to Tom - "Ye know kiddie, I told him - what you've written there; it's bloody impossible!"

When I eventually moved up to Liverpool as leader in 1955, I had barely settled in for about six months when I had a letter from the BBC offering me a post in the Symphony Orchestra to sit on the front desk as co-leader with Paul Beard. George Willoughby, the Orchestral Manager came up and spent a couple of days discussing the pros and cons of the whole situation. It was a tempting offer, both financially and prestigiously for me, still fairly young, to be in a high London position, but in the end I decided that at that stage I needed to prove myself as a leader independently, and having taken that on in Liverpool, it was wrong to change before having made some sort of fulfillment. I still sometimes wonder whether that was the right decision, and what different course my career might have taken, but on balance I think I did the right thing. Still, Paul Beard remains as in many ways an ideal of what a leader should be.

Marie Wilson, as I have said before, was without doubt the greatest female orchestral player of her time. She was a founder member of the BBC Symphony Orchestra at its inception in 1930, and when Paul Beard arrived in 1936, she was firmly established as his number two, and frequently led when he was absent.

Marie was a Tynesider. Her father was a violinist and named her after the great woman violinist Marie Hall, also from Newcastle-on-Tyne. She got her early musical experience by playing for the silent cinema orchestras, where you had to be quick on the uptake and able to read anything. In an era where rehearsal schedules were tight, Marie was never daunted. She was a larger-than-life character with a life-style that ran constantly in top gear. When she came to visit us (which she did frequently) we battened down the hatches and prepared for a lively time.[17] She gave me a lot of confidence when faced with the prospect of the job in Liverpool. If a woman like that thought I was worth helping, then, I felt, I had better try to live up to it. No-one had a bad word to say about Marie, and everyone admired her abilities. She, on the other hand, was pretty intolerant of players who didn't give a hundred percent. "I can't stand those crawlers!" she would explode, meaning people who would never commit themselves to the beginning of a phrase – people in the middle of the section who always waited for others to lead the way - people whose main aim in life was not to make a mistake and not to be found out. As, later in life, she began to be herself in the middle of the section and found out for herself what was actually going on, she became even more vociferous about this and sometimes managed to ruffle a few feathers. But, being a born leader, she also knew how to do this without raising resentment.

Jean Pougnet was a notable leader of the time. I have spoken of him earlier as the one pupil of my teacher Rowsby Woof who made his (Woof's) reputation in the first place. Everyone came flocking along to Rowsby's classes wanting to play like Pougnet.

He led the LPO for a time during the War, and indeed I played with them then on a couple of occasions at the Proms as a student extra. I also played later in film sessions at Denham when Jean was leading, and also did chamber music broadcasts with him. His playing exemplified Woof's ideal that the violin should be like a beautiful disembodied voice. Position changes and bow changes should be always inaudible, and of course intonation must always be impeccable. He was a fine concerto soloist, and there is a marvelous performance of the Delius Concerto available from him, conducted by Beecham. I remember him in the breaks of sessions or rehearsals, never letting the violin out of his hand, and whilst chatting with friends constantly exercising the left hand fingers as if searching for some ultimate perfection.

Thomas Matthews was a similar violinist leader and soloist. He was a student of Carl Flesch, and this itself guaranteed the highest standard. His appearance was lean, elegant and handsome – imagine a serious edition of the comic actor Hugh Laurie. I first saw Tommy when he was leading the LPO during the War, the day after the Queen's Hall was bombed. The orchestral rehearsal was transferred from there to the Duke's Hall at the Academy, and although the students were not allowed to listen to the rehearsal, we had the excitement of mingling with all the players in the canteen during the break. I had the nerve to have a chat with Tommy, and he remembered this when after the war

Further Scrapings

I did a few dates with the Royal Philharmonic Orchestra conducted by Josef Krips[18] I have mentioned previously how Tommy impressed with the taxing solos in "Also sprach Zarathustra" by Richard Strauss. I was bold enough to compliment him, and he gave me a long and interesting chat about the prospects of getting a leader's job.

Tommy was a very fine soloist and gained a high reputation with his performances of the Elgar Concerto. He had ambitions as a conductor and later went on to lead the Scottish Orchestra, on condition that they gave him some conducting experience.

Manoug Parikian I have written about extensively elsewhere. I shall always be grateful to him for the help and encouragement he gave me during various stages of my career. I was in the Philharmonia during almost the whole time that he was leader. He always brought elegance and dignity to his role, over and above the fact that his playing was a model to us all.

He seemed supremely confident, whether on the concert platform or socializing with visiting soloists, conductors or other dignitaries. His English was impeccable, considering he had been brought up as a child in Cyprus, speaking mainly Turkish, though its very perfection betrayed a certain artificiality. This was particularly marked on the few occasions when he allowed himself to swear – it sounded so contrived! I remember, a car-load of us returning from a day's film sessions at Elstree Studios. Hans Geiger was driving, Manoug sat in the front, and in the back were me, Jessie Hinchliffe and Jack Kessler, the number 3 in the fiddle section, a Hungarian who like Manoug spoke English with the exaggerated perfection of an acquired language. During the trip, Jack began a long diatribe directed at Manoug, more or less accusing him of turning a blind eye on lapses of orchestral discipline. "You've no idea what's going on at the back, Manoug. There's too much talking, some slack playing, you must use your authority more. Put your foot down! Show them who's the boss! It's getting far too lax"- and so on and so on. Manoug took it all with perfect composure and dead silence.

It so happened that Manoug was the first person to be dropped off at his destination. The car stopped – he got out, turned to the driver, saying "Thank you very much for the drive, Hans." Then looking over into the back of the car, he rasped out – "And in future, Mr. Jack Kessler, stop trying to lead the orchestra from the fucking second desk" and forcibly slammed shut the door. There was a stunned silence within, then Jack responded in an amazed voice "Well, the ungrateful bastard!"

In actual fact the two of them got on very well together. Jack was possibly equal to Manoug technically and for a brief period they formed a string quartet where they proposed to alternate as leaders. It didn't work, because Jack's perfectionism made him far too nervous in performance.

Manoug's two great idols were Josef Szigeti (1892-1973) and Jascha Heifetz (1901-1987) – two quite opposite types of violinists. He used to hold Szigeti up as the most intellectually satisfying of performers. Though having in some ways an awkward style (some said he looked as if he was playing the violin in a telephone box!) his choice of bowings and fingerings were often of the utmost originality.[19] His many recordings are still valued for their musical qualities, and his writings on violin playing are excellent. Unfortunately his stiffness in style together with a nervous temperament led to a decline in standard of concert performance later in his career. Heifetz, Manoug admired (as we all did) for his immaculate style and technique of an inimitably suave character, and for an absolute single-mindedness in his personality, and intolerance of incompetence in others. Heifetz also admired Manoug. When he performed the Brahms Concerto with the Philharmonia in (I think) 1952 at the Festival Hall, I observed them in close conversation, when Jascha was obviously expressing his thanks and admiration; obvious in spite of the great soloist's characteristic dead-pan expression. When Jascha did briefly smile it was so unexpected and welcome – like a flash of the most brilliant sunshine!

A sad time for all violinists was in December 1987. Manoug wrote a most excellent and moving obituary in the Times for Jascha Heifetz who had died on the 10th. On the 24th of that same month Manoug himself died from a sudden completely unexpected stroke. He was 67, and was deeply mourned by all musicians who knew him.

Further Scrapings

I had intended to confine this chapter to discussing leaders who influenced me to a greater or lesser extent before I myself began leading in 1955. There is one exception I must make however, and that is the legendary leader of the Vienna Philharmonic Orchestra, Willie Boskovsky (1909-1991).

By the time I moved to Liverpool, Boskovsky had retired from the VPO and was making a reputation presenting Viennese Concerts with orchestras world-wide. He came to Liverpool several times, and on each occasion he would give a concert in the Philharmonic Hall, then tour around our usual out-of-town venues. In that way, I got to know him really well, because I used to drive him to the different places,[20] and we would spend up to a week together. He was good company, and loved to talk about his career and background.

Like many other Viennese violinists, he had been a pupil of Arnold Rosé.[21] Boskovsky acquired from him the equal expertise in orchestral playing and chamber music. As was usual in Vienna, promising pupils of orchestral members were given the chance to play in the orchestra, and as a boy Willie was frequently asked to sit with his mentor in rehearsals and concerts. This system is responsible for the unique cohesion in character and style exhibited by the Viennese string players.

The set-up of the Vienna Philharmonic is similar to some other Germanic orchestras, inasmuch as its members are all employed by the State Opera House: they have state salaries and are virtually civil servants. The Opera has a large number of orchestral players on its payroll, so that each person is only required for a certain number of opera performances. This enables the Vienna Philharmonic Orchestra to be established as a self-governing body, whose members are selected from the opera players. It is considered an honour to play in the concerts, and consequently only a small honorarium is paid to players over and above their basic salary. Willie made it pretty clear to me that this was one reason why he left to set up his own touring and recording career, feeling he deserved better financial recognition for his growing fame.

He spoke a lot about Nathan Milstein, whom he admired greatly for the clarity and honesty of his technique and musicianship, and he was proud of the fact that Milstein admired him. Whilst we were together he often played to me. I remember him demonstrating the Joachim cadenzas to the Mozart Violin Concertos which he played with the utmost *elan* and brilliance – no languorous hanging about. Sparkling could best describe it. I was able to play to him, and in effect he gave me quite a few informal lessons.

The concerts were always successful. He communicated easily and directly with the audience and they loved him. He played the Strauss waltzes, marches and polkas with genuine authentic style – none of the exaggerated *rubato* affected by too many others, but just a hint of rhythmic freedom to captivate the listener. He conducted violin in hand, joining in the performance whenever he thought appropriate, though if we performed something like Schubert Unfinished Symphony he would conduct with a baton in the usual way. I remember one rehearsal of this work he was asking for a real *pianissimo* from the violins – ever softer; but in a terse aside to me – "Not you!" He still wanted the leader to stand out, to provide a contour to the sound. This was the kind of thing you could learn from a great performer.

His chamber music recordings with the Vienna Octet are of the highest standard. Both the Schubert Octet and the Mendelssohn Octet are amongst the finest on record, and I have never heard anything to surpass the Schubert Trout Quartet recorded by him with Clifford Curzon. He helped me considerably in choosing repertoire for my own chamber music concerts at the Liverpool Walker Art Gallery, particularly in making me aware of the beautiful String Sextet which forms the overture to the Richard Strauss opera "Capriccio", and makes a most lovely concert item.

In 1963, my family was given the loan of a beautiful Swiss chalet in the village of Loecherbad for a fortnight's idyllic holiday. It belonged to the pianist Margaret Kitchin who had. often played in the Liverpool Musica Viva concerts. Imagine our surprise when Willie Boskovsky turned up, completely unannounced, with his lovely actress wife. It was good to feel the friendship of such an artist and at the same time such a down-to-earth character. Apart from his musical activities, he was a keen sportsman, and it was said that he could easily have become a professional football player. If I was asked to select my best orchestral leader of all times, I think it would have to be Willie.

PM, publicity photo, Liverpool.

Performance of Britten Concerto with topical comment!

Sir John Pritchard recording at EMI Studios Abbey Road with the LPO. In background Ted Parker, LPO orchestral manager and cellist Peter Halling.

Party at the Groves' house after performance of "Child of our Time", 6 February, 1965. Sir Charles, Heather Harper (soprano), Lady Hilary Groves, Johanna Peters (contralto), Sir Michael Tippett (composer).

Telephone
01-935 1367

38, WIGMORE STREET,
LONDON.
W. 1.

October 9th 1970

Dear Peter

       May I thank you for all the preparation, obviously most detailed and thorough, which you had put in before my Elgar rehearsals began. It was indeed a very great pleasure to hear such a splendid performance of the Symphony and I am most grateful.

       I have asked Mr. Wilfred Troutbeck, who is an old friend of mine at Twickenham and does this work professionally, to send you a copy of the record when he gets it next Wednesday.

Many thanks

Yours ever
Adrian C. Boult.

Peter Mountain, Esq.,
Broadcasting House,
Whiteladies Road,
Bristol, 8.

Letter from Sir Adrian after performance of Elgar 1 by the BBC Training Orchestra 1970.

Telephone
01-935 1387

38, WIGMORE STREET,
LONDON,
W. 1.

January 13th 1972

Dear Mr Mountain

    I want to thank you and all your colleagues very heartily indeed for the very fine performances we had yesterday. I really do not think I remember an orchestra that has ever understood more splendidly the spirit and feeling of the Symphony and realized it so well. Would you please thank them all very much indeed?

    I must say a word too about the continuance of the Orchestra. It will be the scandal of the century if it is allowed to disappear now. Under the direction of Mr. Moore and Mr. Rose and your leadership it is going on so magnificently that one simply cannot think of it as having to disappear. I feel certain that some money will be found somewhere and I only hope the decision will be taken soon so that you can go on without any more anxiety.

All good wish. thanks

yours ever

Adrian Boult

Peter Mountain, Esq.,
Broadcasting House,
Whiteladies Road,
Bristol, 3.

Letter from Sir Adrian in support of the BBC Training Orchestra when it was under threat in 1970.

The Prime Minister rehearsing in the Royal Festival Hall.

Sir Edward Heath conducting the BBC Training Orchestra at the Royal Festival Hall in 1973.

10 Downing Street
Whitehall

5 December 1973

Dear Peter Mountain,

    I have written separately to Philip Moore, covering a letter of thanks to the orchestra for all its hard work on the Robert Mayer Carol Concert; but I wanted also to send you a short line to thank you most warmly for all that you did to help me and to give a lead to the players. It was a most enjoyable experience in co-operative leadership; and I hope that you felt, as I did, that the result justified the hard work which all concerned put into it.

With all good wishes,

Yours sincerely,

Edward Heath

Peter Mountain, Esq.

Letter from Sir Edward Heath.

Henryck Szeryng and PM. Rehearsal in Philharmonic Hall for
Bach 2 Violin Concerto, 27 August 1963.

David McCallum by Breta Graham, my colleague in the Boyd Neel Orchestra, about 1949. Sketched on a railway journey.

PM in Bingley 1992, when he received the Honorary Doctorate of Literature from the University of Bradford for services to music education.

Boyd Neel Orchestra in BBC Maida Vale Studio conducted by Georges Enesco, 1950. Maurice Clare (leader), Felix Kok, Ernest Scott, Breta Graham, Max Gilbert (1st viola), Ken Essex, James Whitehead (1st cello), Hilary Robinson, Stanley Mant (standing).

PART III

1955 TO 1966

LIVERPOOL

Chapter 18 – A New Beginning

The period through which we had just passed, from 1947 when I came out of the Marines and started my career proper, up to May 1955 when I realized my ambition and began to lead a major symphony orchestra, was in many ways a period of growth, certainly for me and also for the country. From 1945 to 1951 we had had Attlee's Socialist Government which instigated the Welfare State and the National Health Service, which whatever its present troubles may be, has certainly seen a tremendous increase in life expectancy since it began. There was a surge of reconstruction following Attlee's grateful acceptance during the Truman presidency of aid under the Marshall plan from 1948 onwards. When Churchill was returned to power in 1951, the general mood of optimism continued with the Festival of Britain and the increased growth in reconstruction together with the disappearance of wartime restrictions. One great shadow cast a depression over the general euphoria in the shape of the Korean War from 1950 to 1953. People found this a profound shock – we thought this kind of conflict was a thing of the past, but spirits were kept up by the Coronation in 1953 and the conquest of Everest announced the same day.

The Cold War was in its early stages, though things were growing increasingly threatening. Another ominous event from Britain's point of view was the accession to power in Egypt of Colonel Nasser in 1954. In 1955, Churchill resigned and handed over to Anthony Eden, who in 1956 presided over probably the most disastrous decision made by our country in modern times i.e. the Suez Crisis in 1956, which happened just as we were settling into Liverpool. This seriously damaged the credibility and influence we had, especially with America. For the first part of our Liverpool stay, things did take a more optimistic turn with the Macmillan phrases – "The Winds of Change", and "You've Never Had It So Good". But the last years of the fifties showed a steady intensification of the tension between East and West, culminating in the building of the Berlin Wall in 1961 and the Cuban Missile Crisis of 1962, when there was genuine fear

Further Scrapings

felt throughout the country and indeed the world, that our fate was in the hands of a few vacillating politicians, and if either Kennedy or Khrushchev were to press a button there would be a world-wide holocaust.

However, our family was in optimistic mood early in 1955. Muriel had traveled up before me to see to the purchase of our house from my predecessor Henry Datyner and his wife, Cherry Isherwood, pianist and harpist who had been a student with us at the RAM. It has always happened that Muriel has chosen our living places, quite independently from me. In this case, she inspected the house in Partridge Road, Blundellsands when it was warm, cheery, well-lit and full of a bustling happy family, and was charmed with it. She then had to come back and finish her commitments in London; I went up in May to start the job, but she and the kids couldn't move until November, and in the meantime I lived in the flat of Barrie Hall, the orchestra's Concerts Manager. I didn't have chance to go out and see the new house until late October. When I did, it was a cold, foggy autumn day and I had the shock of my life. The garden looked neglected; the house was empty and gloomy. Marks where pictures had been showed on all the walls; – my first and depressing reaction was "What a dump!" Fortunately, the family's arrival transformed things considerably, and we had eleven happy years in what turned out to be a comfortable and spacious dwelling. The one major snag was that it was just next to the Southport to Liverpool electric railway, and trains went clattering past every ten minutes of the day. It was amazing, though, how you got used to it. You would have thought as musicians we would have found it intolerable, but incredibly enough the only time I remember being aware of the trains was when they had a two-day rail strike and the silence we suddenly found was rather un-nerving!

Domestic life was good in those days. Paul was 6, Alison was 2, and Jeanette came on the scene in November 1956. They all grew up to attend excellent schools just on the doorstep. We were quite near Merchant Taylors Boys School which Paul soon went to, and Alison went eventually to Merchant Taylors Girls Prep. The area was very attractive; with large houses (many much larger than ours) dating rather deplorably from the era of rich Liverpool slave traders. Now, however, Blundellsands (pronounced *Blundellsarnds!*) was definitely the posh part of Crosby. The local joke was that in Blundellsands, sex was what the coal came in. It was one of the original leafy suburbs.

At the same time as Jeanette was born, we got ourselves a dog – Sammy – and he was a lively presence and a lovely companion all through the growing up of our family. I love dogs, Muriel loved dogs, and I am 100% in favour of children growing up with the companionship of these great animals. In fact, I think that now is the place to devote a little chapter to my personal doggie history!

Chapter 19 – Dogs

There is only one drawback to having dogs; that is that they die. The passing of all our dogs have been marked by real sadness, because they become so much a part of your life. Treat a dog well, and he or she will return to you unquestioning love and devotion, will sympathize with all your moods and never criticize you. People say dogs are shameless sycophants – I don't care if they are. I can do with a bit of sycophancy every now and then. The dog tells you that you can do no wrong, and I like that!

Mum and Dad also loved dogs and always had one. The first I can remember as a little boy was Mackie, a rather boisterous Airedale terrier, of whom I was always a bit wary because he could easily knock me down, and he frequently did! However, he was amiable enough, but I didn't get to know him too well before he came to a sad end. His greatest pleasure was to roll on grass – anywhere – the front lawn - the back garden - whenever we went for a walk he just loved rolling on grass. Unfortunately just beside our house were tennis courts, and behind them a very well-kept bowling green. Mackie, if he managed to get out on his own developed a passion for rolling on this bowling-green. However much the attendant shooed him off, he always returned – nothing could stop him. The beautifully manicured grass must have been a special pleasure for him, but it was kept in its state of perfection by the liberal use of chemical fertilizers and weed-killers which had a dreadful effect on poor Mackie's skin. Nearly all his hair fell out; he became terribly ill, the vet found no cure so he had to be put down.

This was very sad, so Dad went prospecting for a replacement. In those days we were not at all well off, so something like Mackie, who had been a thoroughbred, was out of the question. In the end, our local fish and chip shop had a bitch that had produced a large litter, and as regular customers we got our next canine friend as a gift.

This was Jumbo, so called after Jumbo Haddock, a large species of catfish that fish shops often used to buy to cut up into fish portions.

(It is delicious; tastes like good quality cod!) Jumbo was a lovely friendly mongrel – rather beautiful in her own way. As far as we could tell she was a cross between a fox terrier and a Pomeranian. She was black and white, but with lovely silken long hair and a curly tail that went round twice like a double question mark – also a markedly snub nose. A very affectionate creature but again unfortunately rather short lived. She developed distemper – maybe we hadn't had her properly immunized - and sadly died on Christmas Eve 1932, thus completely ruining our festivities.

In the New Year, Dad took me into Bradford for some shopping and we went into the old open-air St John's Market. Sitting in a cage in one of the stalls was a poor little mongrel, mostly white with a black patch over one eye, and not too unlike our dear departed Jumbo. I took one look at it, and wouldn't be satisfied until Dad, not too reluctantly, paid out seven and sixpence and we took it triumphantly home. This was Paddy, who was undoubtably my dog, and lived a long and happy life, up to well after I left home for student days in London. Paddy, like Jumbo, was half a black and white fox terrier, but the other half was probably a bull-terrier, because his one eye surrounded by white hair was decidedly pink, and the hair itself was short and smooth. He was a marvelous companion, and everyone knew and loved him. I often remember taking him for walks all over the district, and people would call out "Hello Paddy!" They didn't know me, but they knew the dog. Before we had a car in the pre-war days, Paddy used to accompany us everywhere, often on the tram that ran past our house from Bradford, then right through to Bingley, about three miles further on. One day, Dad took Paddy on the tram to Bingley where he had various jobs to do. Paddy tagged along with him, then obviously got a bit bored and wandered off. Dad completely lost him; came home very worried and found Paddy curled up asleep in front of the fire. We heard later from one of the tram conductors who we knew, that Paddy had got on in Bingley, stayed peacefully under a seat, and solemnly got off at the right stop, just opposite our house. He didn't even offer to pay!

During my years as a student, and then in the Marines, it was always such a thrill to be reunited with Paddy whenever I came back for a holiday.

When, after the War, we set up house in King Henry's Road, it was not possible to think of having a dog. Our canine pleasures were limited to our visits up North to see the family. When Paddy eventually died, my parents moved up to Eldwick Villas, a lovely isolated whitewashed house backing onto the broad prospect of Ilkley Moor and facing a wide panorama of Airedale. There they had geese, poultry, cats, and of course a dog – a beautiful golden cocker spaniel. I was at the time playing in the Boyd Neel Orchestra so they obviously called him Boyd.

He was the only dog in the Mountain family who had the remotest claim to be musical It was my Dad who started it. One Christmas, by some means or another, he got poor old Boyd to respond to the singing of "Good King Wenceslas" so that whenever we got to "Gath'ring winter" Boyd would join in on the word "fu-u-el" with a howl which traveled up and down a perfect fourth, fitting in perfectly with the singing. It got so that you only had to say "Gath'ring" to Boyd and the great howl of "fu-u-el" would come pealing forth!

Jim was a lovable black Labrador who was really my sister Kath's dog, but who always greeted me as a member of the family, whenever we came to visit. I have always regretted not ever having a Labrador of my own, as they are the most affectionate of dogs. I have read recently that Labradors rank high in the list of dogs that bite people, but I ascribe this to the fact that some people are quite stupid in the way they treat animals, and if a Labrador were to bite you, they could cause damage, as they are powerful creatures.

When we settled in Liverpool and Jeanette had been born, I determined that we needed a dog. I had been disturbed that when we were living in London, Paul developed a real fear of dogs because we didn't have a dog at home. Whenever I took him out for a walk in his baby days, if a dog appeared he would show real panic and burst into tears, and we would have to cross the road to avoid it. Of course, he grew out of that phobia, but now we had a house of our own, I wanted the girls in their early years to have the experience of loving and caring for a fellow creature; our own dog.

I can't remember where we got Sammy from. He was a rather small, nondescript brown mongrel terrier, but he had tremendous character and gave us all great pleasure and companionship over the following sixteen or seventeen years. He wasn't quite as sycophantic as some dogs, and certainly had a definite mind of his own. In fact, one of his last acts was to give me quite a nasty nip when I was taking him to the vet and lifting him out of the car. Nevertheless, he was an integral part of our family from 1956 until we were in Bristol with the BBC Training Orchestra. He was certainly quite a lady's man, and lived life to the full. I was practicing at home one day when the phone rang. It was a near neighbour of ours, a very nice lady rather similar to Penelope Keith in "The Good Life". She answered rather distractedly – "Oh Peter, could you come round? It's Sammy. I don't know what to do. He's, he's *fighting* with Candy". This was their rather pampered Corgi bitch that lived a life of secluded leisure. I dropped everything, jumped in the car and rushed round to their house. I got out – all was quiet – no sign of fighting. I looked in the window and the kids were there, looking rather subdued. They pointed silently round the back of the house, and when I opened the side gate, there was Sammy on top of Candy, stuck in and he couldn't get off! Eventually Cynthia and I had to pour a couple of buckets of cold water over them to effect a separation. The result of this liaison arrived a few months later, a motley litter from a highly bred corgi of eminent lineage, and a little whippersnapper like Sammy. Keith, the husband, really a good friend, but also a very eminent lawyer, said he had been tempted to serve a maintenance order on us!

Sammy lived on, right through our Liverpool days, through the subsequent two or three years back in London, and on into my time in Bristol with the BBC Training Orchestra.

One afternoon, in Bristol, I came home from work to find Muriel and Alison in tears. They had been to the vet with Sammy, and the prognosis had been bad. "Poor little dog, he's getting on and he's got nephritis, severe liver problem – perhaps it would be better just to leave him with us so he doesn't suffer too much". They refused this, and brought Sammy home to give him as much comfort as possible.

At the same time, Bob Chadwick, a violinist in the orchestra, told me his girl friend was a kennel maid at a local establishment which bred Alsatians. Apparently the last litter their prize bitch had produced were all sold except one, and if that was not sold it would have to be put down to make way for the next lot. It was a bitch, and we could have it for an absolutely nominal sum. We went round with Muriel, Alison and Jeanette, and the girls really fell for this gorgeous puppy – we couldn't possibly let it be put down. So, home it came.

The effect on Sammy was magical. Suddenly he had a beautiful woman about the place! Instead of acting the poor invalid, he perked himself up, paraded around like a two year old when we took them for walks, and Minna (named after Wagner's first wife) just adored him. It was incredibly funny when Minna first came on heat a few months later. Obviously we had to keep them strictly apart, one in the kitchen and the other in the scullery. When the door was accidentally opened, there was a great big kerfuffle and they just changed places. They both knew there was something in the other room they really wanted!

But obviously Sammy's days were numbered. I remember the sad day I had to take him to the vet for the last time. The arrangements at that firm were handled incredibly insensitively. I had to bring this poor little body, still painfully breathing, and, in front of a full waiting room, hand him over to a po-faced young girl behind the counter, and then rush out, a grown man, streaming with tears.

Minna grew up to be certainly the most handsome dog we have ever had. Her father was a Crufts champion, and she had the most beautiful expression and a lovely coat. The only problem was that she moulted regularly and when she did, the whole house was full of dog hairs. Muriel used to take her out into the country, go into a field and pull out hair by the handful. When she had finished it looked as if a couple of sheep had been killed.

Talking of sheep, Minna's one failing was that she could not resist chasing sheep. We once let her off the lead when we were camping in our motor caravan at the top of Glencoe, and she rushed off, only reappearing half an hour later I strongly suspect she had killed a sheep. Another time we climbed Pen-y-Ghent, my favourite mountain in North Yorkshire. I finished completely exhausted because I had to keep Minna on the lead the whole time and she pulled to get away continuously because of nearby sheep.

She was very intelligent; the only snag was that if something happened that she didn't understand, she would be incredibly frightened. It could be a balloon or a plane in the sky, or a building under construction and covered with plastic sheeting blowing in the wind. Any other dog would just ignore these things, but poor Minna needed to know, and if the phenomenon was outside her comprehension, she was terrified! There was no doubt about the fear – her teeth chattered! But she was absolutely lovable to all she really knew, and we couldn't possibly have had a nicer natured pet.

Unfortunately, German Shepherds (Alsatians) are not long lived, and aged eleven she began to suffer the ailment that often strikes them i.e. that their bulk is too much for their back legs. When we were in Scotland in 1979, the vet finally came to our house to put her to rest. He was a sensitive man, he knew Minna well, and he wept as he gave her the final injection that put the dear old thing peacefully to sleep.

For a year we were dogless, Muriel vowing we wouldn't have another – it was too much emotional strain. However, at Christmas 1980, Jeanette and John (her then husband) knew we were secretly pining for one, and turned up at our new mansionette in Kew Terrace with a little black bundle, a lovely Border Terrier puppy that we immediately loved. We were then doing a lot of touring around the Hebridean Islands, so we called her Islay (pronounced without the s).

Islay was our companion for the next ten years of our stay in Scotland, and we took her everywhere. In those days we did a lot of touring in the Highlands with our motor caravan, and she came with us. To begin with, she did suffer from a bit of car-sickness which was not good, but she got over that. She had a memorable camping holiday on her namesake island, and endured really tough hikes through thick heather in pouring rain. She survived one very narrow squeak. Muriel was just coming back from a walk with her in the Glasgow Botanical Gardens, just opposite our flat. She had the dog on a lead, but it was unfortunately one of those expanding things. I happened to draw up in the car on the opposite side of the busy Great Western Road; Islay spotted me, and quick as a flash rushed right out into the traffic and was knocked down by a car. She was unconscious, but fortunately the only real damage was a badly broken leg. Our vet did a marvellous job, with a long operation and putting in a metal plate to hold the badly shattered bones together, and she was in the vet's hospital for a week. But after a long spell in plaster she emerged unscathed.

Eventually she fell ill with some complaint that the vet said was rather like human Aids, inasmuch as all her resistance to any disease failed, leaving her completely defenceless to every complaint. She just dropped dead suddenly during our first summer back in Bingley.

Again we had a spell without a dog, but again we were really pining for one. Our new vet, who had looked after Islay in her final days, told us that he had a dog who was injured, and it was suspected had been badly treated. We went to see him and found a poor dejected cocker spaniel, recovering from a car accident after having been attacked by another dog. The vet told us he thought he was about 9 months old. So, when he was better, we took him home and called him Nab, because I was then conducting the Bradford Youth Orchestra and we rehearsed at Nab Wood School.

Nab was probably the most affectionate dog we ever had. He was often rather fearful of other dogs, probably because of past experiences, but he loved people. He grew into a really handsome specimen with beautiful red-golden hair and big brown eyes. All the girls loved him. Unfortunately his tail had been docked. I hate that practice – all that Nab had left was a tiny inch-long stub, which instead of wagging, vibrated at a tremendous rate! It was still very expressive of his feelings, but I used to say that his *vibrato* was too fast!

If Nab had a fault it was that, like his entire breed, he was eternally hungry. Left to himself he would have eaten continuously: you often see rather over-weight spaniels. We kept him religiously to the diet prescribed by the vet, but he always ate his twice daily ration of dog food in ten seconds flat.

One characteristic of all dogs (and certainly of Nab) is that they cannot lie. They are incapable of deceit, and what they are feeling shows up absolutely clearly in their facial expression and body language. I remember one occasion when we had to leave the dog alone in the house for an hour or so for some reason. I made sure that all cupboard doors were closed, no food was around, and there was no mischief he could get into. When we returned, I took one look at the animal and I could see something was wrong Guilt was written large over his whole face and demeanour. "Nab" I grated – "*what* have you been up to?" We soon found out. I went into the dining room, and he had been up on the table where there was a bowl of fruit. He had eaten two lovely ripe pears, most of an apple and an entire banana, including nearly all the skin. The only thing he left untouched was a lemon! It didn't seem to do him any harm, though.

Nab died just after the Millennium, and that was the last of our own dogs. Dog walking was getting too much for both of us, and dogs do need to be walked. It is essential to satisfy the pack instinct in them – to sally forth with the pack leader, a role which the owner assumes, and have a daily hunt, or a daily staking out of territory.

But I am not by any means completely dogless. Since my dear wife died, I am living in the Peak District in a flat which is part of my daughter Jeanette's house. She, in addition to horses, two cats, a rabbit and poultry, has two dogs. One is Jumble, a lovable brown and black mongrel bitch who is described as a Manchester terrier, and the other is Mutley, a little bouncy character who is mostly Jack Russell, with apparently a bit of poodle thrown in, though this doesn't show in his appearance. They are both excellent house dogs, barking furiously at any intruder, particularly the window cleaner whom Mutley specially hates! They always bark whenever the front door opens, but as soon as they see me, or any family member, they stop and put on a face which clearly says "O, I'm *so* sorry. I didn't know it was *you!*" Jumble is the family favourite because she is so docile and ingratiating, and Mutley is the lively one who always gets the blame for anything going wrong, but he's a lovely little character. The one quarrel I have with Mutley is that he hates the postman and the paper-boy, and if the porch door is not closed, shows his resentment at their presumption of intruding into our territory by savaging my daily paper and my post. I have to read round the teeth-marks!

Both the dogs treat me as a respected elderly hanger-on should be treated. They come into my room as visitors, smiling benignly and paying their respects most politely and courteously. Then, after a little, they leave, saying in so many words "Goodbye Grandpa, we'll leave you in peace!" I recently read an article by some learned professor that dogs had the intelligence to understand so-and-so many words. Of *course* they have! Any proper dog owner will tell you that their pets understand practically every word that is spoken. Over and above that, you don't even have to say anything, because they understand every single bit of body language too, and you can't hide your feelings from them.

I have another *ex officio* dog who is Spike, belonging to my other daughter Alison, living in Fife, Scotland, and whom I see when I visit them from time to time. Spike is a rather beautiful long haired collie half-breed, with an especially loving nature, and I feel certain that he always remembers me from past visits and accepts me as a member of the family. Alison and her partner Donald have had two dogs – the first – Lucky – died from some strange virus, but both animals must both share the credit of converting Donald from a person who did not particularly like dogs and was unwilling to allow one into the household into someone who now dotes on their lovely Spike.

I must conclude this chapter with one of my favourite "Shaggy Dog" stories.

A man had a dog who was supposed to be so intelligent he could play poker.

Friends came round, saying – "Is it true? – can he really play poker?"

"Oh yes" said the man – "It's true."

"Well, that's marvelous!" they all said.

"No - not really" was the sad reply.

"Not really? – not really?" they all asked. "Why not really?"

"Well" came the sad reply – "He always wags his tail when he's got a good hand!"

Chapter 20 – Some Thoughts on Conducting

Conductors have taken up a major part of my life, so I would like at this stage to set down some observations concerning the art of conducting and its history.

The first thing one must realize is that orchestral conducting as we know it is the most recent musical activity to evolve. Before the 19th century, musical ensembles were kept together mostly by the joint efforts of the violinist leader and a keyboard player who might often be the composer. The first person to wield a conducting baton is generally thought to be the violinist composer Ludwig Spohr (1784-1859), best remembered now as a violinist, but very highly rated in his day as a composer. Such was his popularity in Victorian times that Gilbert and Sullivan mention him in Act 2 of *The Mikado* in the same breath as Bach and Beethoven. His music has waned in esteem today, but he remains an important influence from the time when string playing was adapting to bigger halls, and orchestras were growing in size and social importance. However, in the early eighteen hundreds, the role of the conductor was still limited to ensuring good ensemble. Mendelssohn when conducting is said to have merely set the performance going, then sitting down quietly in an armchair provided on the podium, he listened approvingly to the playing and joined in the applause at the end.

The composers Hector Berlioz and Richard Wagner were also conductors, and they were the first to write essays on the subject. Berlioz is considered to be the first virtuoso conductor, and Wagner was largely responsible for shaping the conductor's role as one who imposes his own views of the music onto the performance rather than just keeping things together. Louis Antoine Jullien (1812-1860) was the first "pop" conductor, concentrating on light music and making himself the star of the show. Although some regarded him as a charlatan, he was important in the democratizing of concert-going and the instigation of Prom concerts. The first full-time serious conductor was Hans von Bülow (1830-1894) although he had an equal reputation as a concert pianist.

The age of the full-time dedicated conductor did not dawn until the early 20th century. Arthur Nikisch (1855-1922) may well be considered as the father of modern conducting. Nikisch's style was greatly admired by Leopold Stokowski, Arturo Toscanini, Sir Adrian Boult, and Fritz Reiner, among others. Reiner said, "It was he who told me that I should never wave my arms in conducting, and that I should use my eyes to give cues." Sir Adrian Boult once told me that if you could have observed Nikisch conducting in a sound-proof cubicle, you would be able to tell from his gestures what work was he was directing!

Following on, we come to the relatively modern era where we have ample recorded legacy, both in audio and video, of the great conductors' performance. I am eternally grateful to have had the experience of playing under the two who were the greatest influences on modern conducting and orchestral playing – Arturo Toscanini (1867-1957) and Wilhelm Furtwängler (1886-1954). Other "greats" I have been privileged to have worked with are Sir Henry Wood, Sir Thomas Beecham, Sir Malcolm Sargent, Sir Adrian Boult, Otto Klemperer, Herbert von Karajan, Leopold Stokowski, Guido Cantelli. Sir Charles Groves, Sir John Pritchard, George Hurst, Walter Susskind, Rudolf Kempe, Pierre Monteux, Paul Kletzki, Bernard Haitink, Daniel Barenboim, Sir Colin Davis, Norman Del Mar and many more. Today, the virtuoso conductor is a fixture in the musical firmament.

Practically all conductors have emerged from some previous musical activity. They can be broadly divided into keyboard players and orchestral players, and a further subdivision can be made between the piano and the organ, and strings and wind. They all tend to have particular strengths and weaknesses.

The pianists are used to playing complicated music in many parts and of a great range, so they are well equipped to read big musical scores. They are generally good at taking care of every department of the orchestra. They may not be as sensitive to the subtleties of colour available to orchestral instruments, the piano being essentially a monochrome percussion instrument and unable to sustain the tone, but they are sensitive to dynamics, as the piano can produce variety of volume according to the sensitivity of the players' touch. Organists have possibly a superior ability to grasp large orchestral scores, but they sometimes are more lacking than pianists in sensitivity to small nuances. The organist's touch does not affect the dynamics. When conducting, they sometimes treat the orchestra as a vast organ, which they expect will respond automatically to mechanical commands, as if pushing and pulling innumerable stops.

Ex-orchestral player conductors are often more sensitive to the qualities of individual instruments. String players also feel a natural progression from the movement of the bow to the sensitive movement of the baton, being able to lead the way and shape the music; as if playing a concerto not just on a violin but on a whole orchestra. One thinks particularly in this respect of Sir John Barbirolli, whose wonderfully expressive baton could only have developed from the bow movement of a first class string player, which he was.

However, they sometimes are liable to ride hobby-horses. This is particularly the case in string players. A fine violinist, having been obliged to make a living in orchestras surrounded by lesser players, suddenly finds himself in a position of power, and can't resist the urge to put the world to rights. Under his regime, the strings can find themselves the subject of endless violin lessons, which they may well resent, and the wind players are relatively neglected.

But, there is an even more important point to make. Instrumentalists are trained to think of the beginning of the physical movement, either of bow or breath, as the beginning of the sound. This is not the case when conducting. The "ictus" or click of the baton's downbeat is not the point of sound; this occurs during the upward natural rebound of the beat. Guido Cantelli, the great young protégé of Toscanini used to talk about this. He said – "You must not come directly on my beat. I give an indication and you must *calculate* where to place the sound." For a gentle beat it could be perhaps a crotchet before the sound, a firmer beat would be say only a quaver ahead, and a really forceful attack could be a semiquaver or even less in advance. But the actual sound should always be on the rebound. It is neither possible nor desirable to have the downbeat and the sound together.

Sometimes, even orchestral players do not appreciate this. I have often been approached by colleagues complaining about the conductor. "Peter" they say, "For God's sake, tell him to stop beating ahead of us the whole time! We don't know where the bloody hell we are!" Sometimes, members of the audience will say "I don't know how you follow this conductor. His beat seems to bear no relation to what you are playing!" However, just think for a moment of Sir Thomas Beecham, and watch the available videos of his conducting. It does look very strange to the layman, yet there was never a single case of his players complaining about lack of clarity. His beat was never metronomic, but it guided the orchestra with instinct and variety to make the music live. It showed the way.

There are a surprising number of conductors who started as wind players. A supreme example was Rudolf Kempe, one whom I admire greatly, and who originally played the oboe. To pick a few other random examples, Sir Colin Davis was of course a clarinetist, and Norman Del Mar played the horn. Norman is to be specially admired in that he had an encyclopedic knowledge of every single orchestral instrument, so no-one could feel neglected when he was in charge. I sometimes think wind players, with the greater length of their breath, similar to a singer, are superior in thinking long phrases to string players, who have only a short bow to play with.

It is up to orchestral players to appreciate that all successful conductors will have different qualities. Instead of trying to seek out their faults, we need to appreciate their good qualities and use them to get the best performance. There are times when even the finest conductors can be annoying to players, but a feeling of Christian forbearance is sometimes the only solution. The podium is a lonely place, so some sympathy is needed for the man up there, facing eighty or so hostile pairs of eyes. When we had the Conductors' Competition in Liverpool, it was interesting to feel the reaction of the orchestra. There were some competitors who were highly respected orchestral musicians themselves and people expected them to find conducting easy. When they sometimes proved to be fairly incompetent at wielding the baton, you could feel people thinking that the art of beating time is not, after all, so very easy, and maybe deserves some sympathy.

Chapter 21 – Conductors in Liverpool

When I moved to Liverpool, the post of Music Director had just been vacated by Hugo Rignold. As he had been there for several years and as he came back pretty regularly as a guest conductor during my time, I would like to say some words about him as he was a figure who deserves to be remembered.

Hugo Rignold (1905-1976) son of Hugo Rignold, conductor and Agnes Mann, opera singer was born in Kingston upon Thames but spent his boyhood in Winnipeg, Canada. Returning to England as a young man, he studied at the Royal Academy of Music, and then, surprisingly, became a blacksmith for a time. However he was already a very fine violinist. He played with many jazz and dance bands of the day, including Mantovani, Jack Hylton, Fred Hartley and Ambrose. He went on to lead his own London Casino Orchestra right up to the Second World War. Many other well-known players at that time were doing much light music, but his early records of jazz caused some snobbish condescension later in his career (as later happened to André Previn).

While serving in the RAF in 1944, Rignold got the chance to conduct the Palestine Orchestra, now the Israel Philharmonic, and thereafter his career remained within the classical sphere. In 1947 he was a staff conductor at Covent Garden, and succeeded Sir Malcolm Sargent as Chief Conductor in Liverpool. His reign was marked by much strife as he rather ruthlessly sacked many older players and gained the hostility of the Musicians' Union. However, he did much good work.

I don't think Hugo would have agreed with my ideas in the last chapter about the conductor's beat. He was very much a violinist conductor, and players told me that when he was in charge he used to spend ages trying to get them to play directly on the down beat. He would bring the stick sharply down, and rap out "You're late! Again. You're late! Again. Late! Again!....until patience wore out. But he actually had an efficient conducting technique and was a very good concerto accompanist.

I enjoyed working with Hugo and you had to admire his ability. He could be a bit wearing at times, though. When he came back as a guest, he would rehearse the orchestra for five or ten minutes, then throw down his baton with a despairing gesture – What's wrong with you all? What are you doing? Oh, oh, I forget, - yes of course, I've been away from you so long!"

We did one concert with the wonderful Seventh Symphony of Sibelius in one continuous movement Hugo did it very well and the rehearsals seemed to go fine. However, I found it rather dispiriting when just as I was preparing to go on for the Symphony, Hugo leaned over to me, and in his rather sardonic Canadian accent, drawled, "Y'know, Peter, this orchestra *used* to give some *marvellous* performances of this work!"

When Rignold left, Liverpool appointed Paul Kletzki[22], the Polish conductor whom I knew from Philharmonia days, but he could not get a labour permit. The Philharmonic Committee could not make their mind up between the next applicants for the post, so my first year was with two joint conductors, John Pritchard (1921-1989) and the Russian Efrem Kurtz (1900-1995)

Pritchard had invited me to be leader, so I naturally felt the most loyalty to him. He was quick-witted, brilliant musically and knew how to manage people. He was not yet very experienced, and there was more than a suspicion in the orchestra that he was learning his repertoire on them. But he was generally well-liked and respected. He came from a musical back-ground – his father had been a violinist in the LSO, and he was already a repetiteur and assistant conductor at Glyndebourne.

Kurtz, on the other hand, an older man, had a wealth of experience. Born in St Petersburg, he had studied there with Glazunov and Tcherepnin. Later he studied in Riga, Berlin and Leipzig where he worked with Nikisch who later made him his deputy. In 1928 Anna

Pavlova booked him to conduct all her performances up to her death in 1931.

He had been Music Director in Houston and Kansas,USA. His wife was Elaine Shaffer, brilliant American flautist. She played with us while Kurtz was there, and also recorded the Bach B minor Suite with Menuhin and the Bath Festival Orchestra. She was a lovely person; a keen keep-fit enthusiast who went everywhere possible by bike. Tragically she died quite young, whereas Efrem, who never seemed to care for himself at all, lived on to be 95!

Efrem was an entertaining figure, but with quite a whiff of the charlatan about him. His favourite trick was to play "The Stars And Stripes" as an encore, and whilst the brilliant piccolo *obligato* was playing he would waltz off the stage, waving his baton cheerfully and leaving us to it. This always brought the house down. In appearance he was lean, tall and willowy with a mop of white hair which always had a discreet blue rinse, like an elderly dowager duchess. He was unfortunately prone to conducting works from memory when he didn't really know them, which we hated. He had various tips and maxims that I always remember. He said you should never end a programme with Dvorak's "New World Symphony" because of the last chord. This is a strong attack by the brass which dies away in a long *diminuendo* to nothing. "Very bad" he would say – "It kills the applause stone dead!"

He had been for a time conductor of the Monte Carlo Orchestra and was quite a gambler. He told me that he kept a separate bank account in Monaco, and that over the years it had grown considerably. I tended to believe him as he was a cunning old fox. His charisma was certainly good for audience numbers, but the orchestra breathed a collective sigh of relief when at the end of the season, Pritchard was confirmed as Conductor in Chief and I began seven very happy years under his direction.

In the last months of 1956 there occurred an event of international importance which affected us all in various ways.

Further Scrapings

The Hungarian Revolution of 1956 was a spontaneous nationwide revolt against the Stalinist government of Hungary and its Soviet-imposed policies, lasting from October 23 until 10 November 1956. It began as a student demonstration which attracted thousands as it marched through central Budapest to the Parliament building.

The revolt spread quickly across Hungary, and the government fell. Thousands organized into militias, battling the State Security Police (ÁVH) and Soviet troops. Pro-Soviet communists and ÁVH members were often executed or imprisoned, as former prisoners were released and armed. Impromptu councils wrested municipal control from the Communist Party, and demanded political changes. The new government formally disbanded the ÁVH, declared its intention to withdraw from the Warsaw Pact and pledged to re-establish free elections. By the end of October, fighting had almost stopped and a sense of normality began to return.

But after announcing a willingness to negotiate a withdrawal of Soviet forces, the Politburo changed its mind and moved to crush the revolution. On 4 November, a large Soviet force invaded Budapest. Hungarian resistance continued until 10 November. An estimated 2,500 Hungarians died, and 200,000 more fled as refugees. Mass arrests and denunciations continued for months thereafter. By January 1957, the new Soviet-installed government had suppressed all public opposition. These Soviet actions alienated many Western Marxists, yet strengthened Soviet control over Central Europe, cultivating the perception that communism was both irreversible and monolithic.

This attracted widespread sympathy in the West, and much effort was made to raise funds for the Hungarian Refugees. As I have told elsewhere, the Liverpool Orchestra gave a Conductorless Concert as a novelty event to raise money for the Lord Mayor of Liverpool's Relief Fund. Bela Siki, a Hungarian pianist already a regular soloist with us, took part in this, and we began to attract other fine soloists, such as pianists Geza Anda, Andor Foldes, Tamas Vasary and Mindru Katz. But more significantly the Hungarian influx provided us with some very fine guest conductors.

László Somogyi (1907-1988) came to the Philharmonic for some concerts in February 1962. He made a strong impression on us, particularly with the Brahms Fourth Symphony, my favourite of the four. But an even more gifted Hungarian had conducted us in November 1960, strangely enough in the same Brahms Symphony. This was the much younger. István Kertész (1928-1973) who was already in demand on the Continent. He had earlier been a protégé of László Somogyi.

István Kertész's concert with us marked his debut in Britain. He was immediately snapped up by the LSO who recorded with him a complete cycle of Dvorak Symphonies, which are still a benchmark for subsequent recordings. He then went on to greater heights, so much so that when we sought to re-engage him for the next season, he was already beyond our budget. A truly outstanding talent; he reminded me strongly of my colleague Granville Jones – the same Celtic intensity, giving the feeling that he could see into things much more intensely than the rest of us.

Tragically, like Granville, he died young. On April 16, 1973, while on a concert tour, István Kertész drowned while swimming off the coast of Israel at the holiday resort of Herzliya. I am certain that had he lived a normal lifespan he would have been one of the greatest international figures in music. As it is, despite a long list of recordings, he is almost forgotten.

A remarkable conductor we had in 1957 was the young Italian Pierino Gamba. Born 1937 in Rome, he was conducting at the age of 10; in fact on u-tube you can see a video of him directing a confident performance of Beethoven 5th Symphony at that age. He was with us aged 20, and there was no doubt that he was already a confident operator. He had already recorded much for Decca, accompanying many eminent soloists such as Ruggiero Ricci. I became quite friendly with him and he came out to our house several times. He had been trained as a violinist but could play the piano to some extent. He had the kind of talent that was immediate – he could do anything if he really tried. One afternoon he wanted to make some music with me, so we had fun bashing through a whole pile of violin sonatas. Eventually we came to the César Franck. The difficult beginning

Further Scrapings

for piano of the second movement was really way beyond him, but after making a complete mess of it, he gritted his teeth, said grimly "Come on, Mr. Gamba; come on – really try!" - psyched himself up and dived in; and it didn't sound too bad!

Another of my favourite visitors was the French conductor Georges Tzipine who came in 1959. We did much Debussy and Ravel with him which were his strong points. He was a charming person, married to an attractive lady who was from Yorkshire. Consequently his typical Gallic accent when speaking English was tinged with a trace of Northern inflexion. He used to say – "Ah yes, zat ees luvvley!" He used to boast that he was the only man in the world to have been married in Paris and had his honeymoon in Sheffield!

Chapter 22 – Bristol

In 1966 we left Liverpool and spent two years in London when I led the second violins in the LPO and played for two seasons at Glyndebourne. However, in 1967 I was offered and accepted the post of Concertmaster of the newly formed BBC Training Orchestra, and the family moved to Bristol where we had a happy and fulfilling time for the next eight years.

The BBC Training Orchestra was originally started in 1965 as a *quid pro quo* between the Musicians' Union and the BBC. The Corporation wanted more "needle time" i.e. hours of the day they could play records without the expense of live music. In return the Union demanded that they do something to help young musicians. The result was the brain-child of Sir William Glock (1908-2000) who was Controller of BBC3 from 1959 to 1972. It was to be a post-graduate orchestra where young talented instrumentalists would learn about ensemble playing, produce regular broadcasts and public performances, and work under first class conductors and coaches.

For the first two years, Leonard Hirsch was in charge. However, he was a violinist leader, not a trained conductor, and he was not willing to play with the orchestra. So the BBC decided to appoint someone to lead the strings, to coach the orchestra and to conduct occasionally. Glock told me during my interview for the job, that the idea had come to him from Leopold Stokowski. The principal was, that it is better to lead by example than to teach, an idea that appealed to me. I was to have the title of Concertmaster, implying something a little more than just leader.

The orchestra was also to have a principal conductor and regular visiting guest conductors. It was based in Bristol so that the players should not have the distraction of the possibility of free-lance work in London. The choice was good because Bristol is the only major British city without a resident orchestra. Philip Moore was the BBC Head of Music for the Western Region, and he was overall in charge of administration and artistic policy. The members of the Orchestra were admitted after audition, and were accepted for a minimum of one year and a maximum of three years. This meant that after their initial year, players had two years to find a suitable more permanent job. At the same time, the more experienced people would be playing with the next-year newcomers, helping to give them experience and confidence, and giving a valuable feeling of continuity.

In the early days, we broadcast regularly from the Colston Hall, Bristol. Chamber music was strongly encouraged, and there were regular visits from the Amadeus String Quartet which was wonderful for the strings. Eminent woodwind and brass players came to coach as well, and I must say that we worked really hard to provide an interesting and stimulating schedule. All the past members I have met later in life have expressed genuine appreciation of their time in Bristol. I wish I could give individual thanks to all who I met in those days. Many have become close personal friends, like Les Child, highly talented violinist who was there when I first took the job, and who has been a valued colleague ever since. I have met players in every part of the country, and several on a recent visit to Australia, who all speak warmly of their time in Bristol

Although I loved the work and supported the idea of such an orchestra, mistakes were made. Glock was an idealist and he did not want it to be a second choice for young players but rather a desirable place to go after finishing Music College. To this end he made the salary equal to those of the provincial BBC orchestras and the Hallé, Liverpool and Bournemouth. This created instant resentment and outrage. I was in Liverpool then and felt the full blast of it. "These kids, fresh out of College, getting all this coaching, not working half as hard as we do and getting the same money! Disgusting!" It was true, for a time, that the Training Orchestra was well off and the others were bringing up families on little more than a pittance. However, it did not last. We were in a period of high inflation. The main orchestras, by agitation and Union negotiations were able to keep up with their living standards, but the young players stayed the same, and within a short time had less than the equivalent of a University grant.

Criticism was constantly being heard. The performance standard of the orchestra was very good, and youthful enthusiasm led to some concerts way above the ordinary routine level. Still, because of the continually changing personnel, it was not always possible to maintain the consistency expected from a regular orchestra. Snide remarks were circulated about the "BBC Straining Orchestra", which were less than ideal for the players' morale.

Still, I never felt there was any lack of loyalty from the members. When the orchestra was threatened with closure, and we had to accept the compromise of changing to be the Academy of the BBC, the players were in the forefront of the battle, and I must say that by contrast, support from the Union was decidedly lacking. It was a very bad step to cut the orchestra down. What the young players needed was experience in the big symphonic repertoire, and instead they had to play revealing classical and Baroque music plus demanding modern chamber orchestra music in direct competition with bands like the ECO and the Academy of St. Martins-in-the-Fields, containing the best players in the country.

Chapter 23 – Conductors in Bristol

The first chief conductor we had was Meredith Davies (1923-2005) who had been and always remained a great friend of mine. He was known as a champion of British music, and directed the first performance of Benjamin Britten's "War Requiem" in Coventry Cathedral in May 1962 in collaboration with the composer. He was particularly keen on the music of Delius, and I was privileged to broadcast the Violin Concerto with him and the Training Orchestra.

Meredith never really had the success he deserved. He was a first class musician; he seemed to be quiet and reserved, but he was capable of directing the largest ensemble with spirit and energy. We put on a concert in the Colston Hall of Walton's "Beshazzar's Feast" with the Training Orchestra, using a number of West Country choirs combined together. They were supposed to have been thoroughly prepared previously, but when we began rehearsals, Meredith found to his horror that they were pretty useless. He was outraged. His usual pleasant demeanour disappeared. They were faced with a raging monster who more or less terrified them into getting the notes learnt, and the eventual performance was first rate, due entirely to his absolute determination.

On another occasion, I remember rehearsing Schubert's Second Symphony. This is not difficult music, but it is most beautiful and demands subtle and sensitive playing. He rehearsed it to the limits of the players' patience, and made them realize what it is to produce real music making, rather than a routine read-through.

He had a dry sense of humour; he looked at the world always with a quizzical twinkle in his eye, and he would not suffer fools gladly. He had started as an organist and choir-master, but had a natural sympathy for all instrumentalists. His beat, whilst not being over-demonstrative was always clear and you knew you were dealing with a real musician.

He was followed by Norman Del Mar (1919-1994), an equally fine musician but different from Meredith in almost every way. Norman was always larger than life, physically and in every aspect of his demeanour. His presence on the podium was sometimes quite overwhelming, prompting wits to dub him (after the large-scale choral work by Delius) "A Mass of Life". He was very good for the orchestra and we did many excellent performances with him. Norman was always perfectly prepared; whether it be a Beethoven symphony, a tone poem by Strauss, or the most obscure modern composition, he would know every note, every detail, every nuance, every little problem encountered. If he had a fault, it was that sometimes he tended to rehearse things that didn't really need rehearsing, raising problems to which everyone knew the answer, instead of trusting the players more.

My friend Manny Hurwitz was a master at encapsulating things with a quick epigram – rather like Groucho Marx. A crowd of us were chatting about various conductors and someone mentioned Norman. "Norman is very very good" said Manny. "The trouble is; he's a bit like a Sherpa guide. He's marvellous on Everest, but you don't really need him on Snowdon!"

However, he was a vastly underrated conductor and musician. His monumental three volumes on the life and works of Richard Strauss are great achievements. The writing is idiomatic and entertaining; just to read a few pages, you can almost hear Norman talking. It seems to be the normal thing to award eminent British conductors with knighthoods, and I feel strongly that both my friends above deserved this honour.

Norman was with the Orchestra during the time its existence was threatened and it was eventually cut down to chamber orchestra size and re-christened The Academy of the BBC. He resisted this fiercely and so did I, but to no avail. The powers that be would not make the funds available and we were fighting a loosing battle.

We had regular excellent guest conductors, which was good, to give the players experience in adapting to different styles. George Hurst had a marvellous empathy with the young players and taught them a lot. His strong personality and uncompromising attitude appealed to them when sometimes it could be annoying to older musicians.

Further Scrapings

I have always admired him greatly. Another regular visitor was Walter Susskind, whom the kids loved. He always arrived with an appearance of wonderful sartorial elegance, and a different but always extremely glamorous lady friend. He was a great, instinctive musical personality.

Edgar Cosma was a Roumanian conductor who had been a protégé of Constantin Silvestri. At the time he was doing a lot of work with the BBC Ulster Orchestra in Belfast, so he came to us as a guest quite often.

He was very good and worked well with the orchestra. However he was often subject to typical Slavic melancholy and one had to be ready to cope with his varying moods. On one occasion he was due to visit us, and I noted that the programme included the Symphony by Georges Bizet, a lovely little work, but containing some really tricky passage-work for the strings, especially in the last movement. So, during the previous week, I arranged a couple of sessions to go through the difficult bits of the Symphony and make sure they all knew what was coming.

On the Monday morning, I met him at the studio. His first words were-

"Mr. Mountain, I must tell you, I am very worried."

"Edgar, why is that?"

"Well, we have this Bizet Symphony. It is very difficult. They will find it difficult. We will have to work hard, to get it in good order; it will stretch their capabilities – I know how it will be. I hope we have enough time."

"Well, maybe Edgar, it won't be too bad."

"No- no, you are wrong. I know; it will take much time. I am very worried."

So, we went into the rehearsal and started the Bizet Symphony, and more or less went straight through it with just a couple of pauses.

We came off for the interval and sat down for a cup of coffee. Edgar turned to me –

"Mr. Mountain, I am very worried." I replied "Whatever for? What's the problem now?"

"Well" he said "this Bizet Symphony; it is not *so* difficult. We have all this rehearsal time. How are we going to fill it all in?"

Edgar was a very precise elegant person, always immaculately dressed. He had one strange peculiarity. He wore spectacles, and instead of putting the arms over his ears in the usual manner, he put them outside his ears, thus compressing them into his head. This gave him a very odd appearance when you looked him in the face.

He also had one characteristic which at first I did not like to ask him about. It was impossible to ignore when he wielded the baton that the first phalange of his right hand index finger was missing. Eventually, he did tell me the story. As a youth he had been all ready to adopt a career as a virtuoso pianist. However, he visited an aviary of tropical birds. He put his finger towards the bars of a parrot's cage, and it bit him. Something similar to psittacosis set in and he lost the top part of his finger. Piano playing was no longer a possibility, so it was then that he took up conducting.

Louis Frémaux was at that time conductor of the Birmingham Orchestra and he came to us for a few concerts. I found him quite a brilliant musician. One of my favourite composers is Francis Poulenc, and of his works I am especially fond of the Concerto for Organ, Strings and Timpani. We did this twice with Frémaux, including a concert in Birmingham Town Hall, and the performances were the best I can remember of this wonderful piece. He was a fine conductor, and it is a pity that his memory has been somewhat eclipsed by being followed in Birmingham by the brilliance of Sir Simon Rattle.

We had a memorable concert and broadcast from the Colston Hall when the Orchestra was combined with the BBC Welsh Orchestra for a performance of Sir Michael Tippett's "Concerto for Double String Orchestra". This work, written in 1938-39 is one of the composer's finest creations and ranks amongst the greatest British string compositions. Tippett himself came to conduct us on this occasion. It was wonderful to be directed by this great composer, but it must be said we had quite a struggle, because he was not by any means a competent conductor. He was a most lovely person and a wonderful musician, but unfortunately instead of giving us a firm beat, he merely indicated the notes, which in a work like this, full of complicated syncopated rhythms is worse than useless. However, because of the respect we all had for this great figure, the performances were pretty successful.

There were many other excellent guests we had and it is not possible to mention them all. However, I cannot ignore the two visits we had from Sir Adrian Boult

The first was when he conducted "Job, a Masque for Dancing" by Vaughan Williams, and I have written about this previously. However, even more memorable was the occasion in January 1972 when Boult conducted us in the Elgar First Symphony.

It was rather like the episode with Edgar Cosma. Boult arrived in Bristol, obviously thinking that the young orchestra had probably bitten off more than it could chew. But I had taken the precaution of preparing the work pretty thoroughly the week before, and when Sir Adrian found they knew the notes quite well, he was delighted and from then on trusted them absolutely. He wrote me a letter afterwards, saying –

"I really do not think I remember an orchestra that has ever understood more splendidly the spirit and feeling of the Symphony and realized it so well. Would you please thank them all very much indeed?

I must say a word too about the continuance of the Orchestra. It will be the scandal of the century if it is allowed to disappear now. Under the direction of Mr. Moore and Mr. Rose and your leadership it is going on so magnificently that one simply cannot think of it as having to disappear."

One final episode I must recall from Bristol days.

On December 1st 1973, the Orchestra gave one of the Robert Mayer Concerts at the Royal Festival Hall, London, and the conductor was none other than the then Prime Minister, the Right Honourable Edward Heath. This was in the middle of the Winter of Discontent, when the Government was in big trouble, with strikes by the miners and every kind of trouble brewing. All the more amazing that Heath could calmly take two days off from matters of state to indulge his passion for conducting and love of music. He spent one whole day the previous week rehearsing with us in Bristol, and then two days later did the concert in London.

Heath had been an organ scholar at Cambridge and was passionately fond of music. He had conducted the LSO on quite a few occasions, but you could not take him too seriously as an orchestral director. Of his extra-political activities, I am pretty sure that he was much better skippering his yacht than conducting a symphony orchestra. The programme we did with him was mostly of Christmas Carols, but it did include a Handel Organ Concerto with John Birch as soloist and began with the Overture to *La Cenerentola* (Cinderella) by Rossini. Starting this is quite tricky for any conductor; after a few rather shaky attempts, Heath turned to me, saying – "Ahem – I think the best thing is if you give a good lead, and I – well – I'll join up with you when you get going"

We had an enjoyable day's rehearsal in the Bristol studio. The programme was to be introduced by the well-known BBC personality Richard Baker, a keen musician, and he was also there for the rehearsals. At lunchtime, Philip Moore took us into the BBC Club for a welcome drink and refreshments. Heath accepted with alacrity a large schooner of sherry, saying with heartfelt feeling – "This'll wash the coal dust away!" Richard Baker leaned over to me with a whispered aside – "One for your memoirs eh Peter?"

Unfortunately, Boult's good wishes for the future of the Orchestra were not fulfilled. The writing was on the wall when Sir William Glock left the BBC in 1972 and shortly afterwards my contract was only renewed one year at a time. In 1975 I was offered the post of Head of Strings at the

Royal Scottish Academy of Music and Drama, so a new life opened for us in Glasgow, of which I have written quite fully in my previous book.

Appendix I
How I Teach

This article appeared in the June 2007 issue of "News & Views", the journal of the European String Teachers' Association, British Branch.

I was brought up from earliest days in an atmosphere of music teaching. My Mum and Dad started to teach professionally and full time when the Great Depression of 1929 destroyed the Yorkshire wool-sorting business that had supported them comfortably until then.

Mum taught piano and started me off at the age of 5, and Dad taught violin, which I began two years later. They both had excellent previous tuition; Mum from a pupil of Tobias Matthay and Dad from the great Arthur Willie Kaye who taught in Huddersfield and had studied with Otokar Ševčík. Kaye had been asked to stay on as Sevcik's chief assistant, but had opted to return to Yorkshire where he produced a long list of Northern violinists, including Laurence Turner (leader of the Hallé) Jessie Hinchliffe (co-leader of the Philharmonia and married to Alan Rawsthorne), Jane Marcus and many others. His work was publicly appreciated by Barbirolli as a deciding factor in the reputation for fine string sound that Sir John produced when he took over the Hallé orchestra in 1943.

Lessons with Dad began when I was seven, and continued until the age of fifteen. Dad was not a highly gifted player, but he was someone who was a force to be reckoned with, and thought very deeply and sincerely about all things violinistic and musical. So much so that I always felt compelled to argue with him! Looking back, that probably wasn't a bad thing, but also looking back I now realise he was very

Further Scrapings

often right. Of course, that was what was most annoying about him! He took over Kaye's principles, based on Ševčik, and a growing awareness of the ideas of Carl Flesch, and applied them with rigour and almost puritanical severity. The path of the bow must follow an unyielding pattern of perfection; the left hand must be drilled with regular finger-swinging exercises by Alexander Bloch – (which I grew to hate!) - but were excellent for developing sheer technical dexterity, and for accuracy of finger placement. Left hand fingers must be kept down whenever possible, and stance must be perfect at all times.

There was great emphasis on the development of what Pa described as the intresor muscles. I realise now that he just invented this word, and he should have referred to the flexors, the extrinsic muscles of the hand that start below the forearm and work in conjunction with the interosseus and lumbrical muscles to bend and stretch out the digits. The names of the complicated muscular set-up of the hand's construction are not important to us. The practical consideration that we as string players have to be aware of is that it is not only the up and down movements of the fingers we must develop, but also the in and out stretching between the fingers, which governs the crossing from string to string and also the stretching and contraction up and down the string vital to the sensitive control of intonation. This ability to move the fingers sideways in every direction is not a natural facility and it is something that any string player has to develop either consciously or unconsciously.

It was a great advantage to be made aware of this at an early stage, and to realise that a lot of sheer hard physical work is needed to enable the hand and fingers to cope with the actual physical demands of playing the violin.

Even the most talented and gifted players have made real concentrated effort over a long period to gain their commanding technique.

Someone like Michael Rabin spent years doing eight hours a day hard practice, at the behest of a domineering mother – his outstanding technique didn't appear without considerable travail. I have just read a book about the life of Walter Legge, the great recording entrepreneur and founder of the Philharmonia of which I was a member in the early days. He recollects that he and his wife (Elizabeth Schwartzkopf) shared an apartment with David Oistrakh and his wife for a time, and each morning began with the great violinist striding up and down in his bedroom, still in his pyjamas, vigorously practising scales and finger exercises. Sportsmen are the same. You have to persevere with exercising the muscles to keep up the highest standards. Excellence in any physical activity entails the often un-natural adaptation of the body's physical make-up, and is only maintained by dedicated regular physical routines. I have known many highly talented players who never realised their potential because they lacked the necessary dedication and determination to persevere in this way. The reverse is often the case. Hard work can transform a less talented person far beyond what first seems possible. So, a good teacher must have the ability and personality to inspire pupils to work and to enjoy it. Without that, there is not much hope of success.

Not only must we be able to do this, but also we must be very clear what we want students to work at.

At the purely physical level, speed and fluency are needed in all the actions, but above all we want accuracy in the control of muscular reflexes, only obtainable in the first instance by slow and careful practice. Exercises that accustom the fingers to operate either a semitone, a tone or a tone and a half apart are essential, as the muscles thus involved are hardly used in normal life. Even more important are exercises for crossing the strings. Because of the fact that the fingers of the left hand are at an oblique angle to the strings, the transit from one string to another involves a complicated motion, which is neither just in and out or just sideways, and must also be supplemented and supported by freedom and motion of the entire arm. So often have

Further Scrapings

I observed good intonation on one string deteriorate terribly when string crossing is involved. The tendency is to neglect the sideways motion that occurs in string crossing, so moving to a lower string results in sharpness, and conversely to a higher string the pitch tends to go flat. In fact, moving accurately from string to string is a kind of knack, which once you get it, feels absolutely simple, but to begin with seems impossible. Good teachers can impart knacks!

As early as possible, there must be practice in double stopping – particularly the playing of thirds. My teacher at the RAM, Rowsby Woof, used to insist that at every lesson we should do some work on Wilhelmji's Book of "Thirds". This I believe is out of print now, but it is an invaluable aid in rational left hand practice. My greatest teacher, Sascha Lasserson, also had a simple thirds exercise which he made us all do and which I passed on to my students. Thirds help to train the fingers, and to train the ear.

The reason that thirds on the violin are confusing for beginners and need a special skill in co-ordination is that the stretching and contracting needed to move between a major and a minor third is the opposite from what feels natural. A major third is produced with a narrow interval between the fingers, a tone and a half apart, and a minor third is wider, with the fingers two tones apart. You have to contract for the wide-sounding interval and expand for the narrow-sounding minor interval, which initially feels unnatural. Obviously, this is because the lower note is produced by the higher finger and the converse being that the higher note uses the lower finger. The opposite is the case with 6ths, which is why people find them so much easier. With them, a minor 6th is narrow (fingers a semitone apart) and you move them a tone apart to play a major 6th.

Peter Mountain

Thirds and Sixths

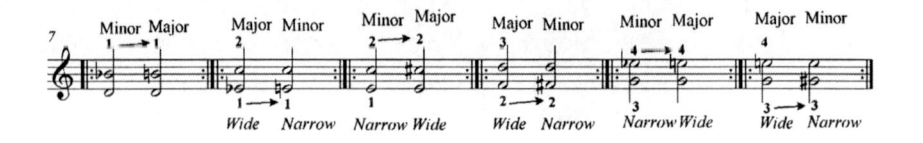

This, of course, is obvious when you think about it, but it is amazing, looking back to my student days, that no one ever pointed this out to me. Playing thirds is a knack, which you have to get into your reflexes, but it is much easier to acquire if you have the logic of them clearly in your mind. I find students get the hang of double-stopping much quicker if this simple idea is made clear.

Together with work on the left hand, there must of course be work on the bowing arm. Good instruction should be given on the bow hold, on encouraging relaxation and flexibility in all movements and good control over the placement of the bow on the string. Lasserson always insisted that we should all spend some time each day on slow bowing, with a beautiful even sound, and with carefully graded crescendos and diminuendos. I would also advocate any exercises or etudes that encourage good bow distribution. The commonest fault, even in reasonably competent players is a lack of facility or a reluctance to use the lower part of the bow. Observe for yourself a typical orchestral string section. You can easily pick out the better players by the freedom of movement in their bowing and ease of approach to the heel. Some players seem to have a sort of limiter in the arm action that inhibits movement up the bow. A good idea is to ask people to play a study or piece in continuous semi-quavers well-known to them, and to move gradually from the heel to the point and back, maybe once every four bars, without the change being audible. In addition, variations in bowing patterns can be applied to such music. My father made me go through pages of Sevcik's forbidding Bowing Technique books, but they can easily become deadly boring. Like strong medicine, they should only be taken under doctor's orders!

The inevitable result of a regime such as that was inevitably some tension, lack of freedom and not a lot of tonal beauty. On the other hand, there was much for which I am still grateful. It incorporated the work ethic into my awareness from an early age. I felt I was striving for something that was worthwhile but wouldn't necessarily come easily.

Dad was constantly quoting the example of great players from the past that fired my imagination. I think that many teachers could do more in this respect. Working with youth orchestras and coaching young players I have often been struck by their relative ignorance of the great violinists of days gone by, the history of the violin – an entrancing study in itself – and the traditions of string playing and teaching. The kids who are going to do well mostly do have this kind of interest. I particularly remember one boy I taught at Douglas Academy in Glasgow, which has a special school for talented musicians. I used to teach him sometimes in the room he boarded in at the school, and the walls were covered not only with pictures of footballers from Celtic, but also of famous violinists, and he read the Strad as avidly as he devoured the sports pages of the Glasgow Herald. He is now a highly successful professional violinist.

My father's rigorous regime had one flaw. It depended on the imposition of strict limits and disciplines on how the left hand and the bowing arm should look. When I finally escaped his influence as a sixteen-year-old to study at the RAM with Woof, I began to think for myself more, and saw from the example of talented contemporaries that there was more than one inflexible way to play. For example, I had always been told to develop strength and energy in the left hand, and I remember Rowsby, trying to get a bit more fluency into my playing, snarling at me "Don't *stamp about* so much, boy!" However, I do remember that my finger co-ordination was proving its worth. Another thing my Dad's legacy left me with was a good ability to keep fingers down and to change position logically. Too many people have such an over-riding concern for continuous vibrato that they never have more than one finger down at a time. The tendency is to hop from one note to the next with a lack of awareness of measuring the exact distances. Ruggerio Ricci puts it very well when he said- "You don't jump about the violin, you crawl about it!" I was made very aware from the first lessons involving position changes of the importance of the subsidiary note – the note that links by a slide up or down to the arrival note. Invaluable practice for this is found in Kreutzer Study No. 10.

On the subject of position changes, I think it is vitally important to get early fluency in the 2nd, 4th and 6th positions. Players lacking strong basic training tend to use nothing but the 3rd, 5th, and 7th positions, what were known as the whole shifts in Leopold Mozart's "Violin Playing". The in-between positions were called half shifts, and are often avoided instinctively by many players, even today. The reason for this is that moving up through the whole shifts means that the same fingers play on the lines and spaces of the stave, thus giving a sense of security in reading music. However, I am certain that facility in particularly the 2nd and 4th positions is invaluable in a great deal of music. This is very much the case in flat keys. Fingerings in older editions of violin music often ignore the so-called half shifts completely, which is a great pity. Students should be encouraged from earliest days to take an intelligent interest in fingerings. It is such an easy way out for pupils to come along with some music, saying, "Oh please will you finger this for me!" Ideally, we should never do this, without the student being there to offer suggestions and being made to realise why the choices of fingering are made. There is never any exclusively right or wrong fingering – I am constantly reviewing my own fingering of music, but I try to be very clearly conscious of the reasons for my latest decisions.

Of course, it is very important to encourage an awareness of tonal beauty in young players, but I think we are growing away from the era where the ideal is a constant luscious tone quality. The myth grew up during the 20th century that one should have a continuous vibrato over the whole tone production, like jam on bread. The start of this tendency has been attributed to Fritz Kreisler and other early 20th century virtuosos. It is true that the great Austrian player had a magnificent and seductive quality of sound, but it is not true that if you vibrate perfectly evenly you'll sound like Kreisler. As with all the great players, his vibrato *meant* something, and careful study of his records reveals a beautiful sensitivity to the changing musical moods, produced by much more than just an unvaryingly seductive tone. Actors can show by a sudden change of vocal intensity the importance of a single word, so can we change the emotional content of a note at the peak of a phrase.

Very interestingly, Mozart mentions vibrato, saying that the human voice vibrates naturally and this should be welcomed, but must not be exaggerated. He goes on to say that exactly the same applies to the tone of string instruments. So much for the authentic performance authorities who seem to imply that vibrato is essentially sinful, and was absent in the ideal atmosphere of pre-romantic music!

One problem with vibrato is that less talented students find it difficult to produce at all, and the more they strive to vibrate, the more they become tense, anxious and frustrated. They often end up with an unattractive nervous quiver, which once acquired becomes almost impossible to eradicate. Talented people generally find they can easily produce a smooth regular wrist movement that gives an attractive relaxed quality to the tone, and we are so pleased with this that we welcome it with open arms. We then leave it unchanged in every kind of music. Speaking personally, I must admit that as a youngster I did not have an immediate facility in vibrato. I found it very difficult, and listened enviously to fiddlers who could effortlessly produce this lovely sound. My vibrato when it did arrive was basically an arm vibrato. However, I was thrilled to read in Carl Flesch that in his opinion vibratos were mainly either wrist or arm, and the latter, although not as natural, often produced a more varied and interesting sound. This is because the speed and, as it were, the temperature of the vibrations can easily be varied by injecting more or less tension into the relevant muscles. Having come to vibrato the hard way, I feel perhaps more aware of the subtleties and changes in mood that it can produce. The violin is a beautiful instrument when sounding anywhere in the vast spectrum, stretching from completely pure *non-vibrato* (maybe in the third movement of Beethoven Quartet Op.132, a sublime expression of thanks for recovering from a serious illness), to the gypsy excitement of something like Sarasate's "Zigeunerweisen". Purists will say that the same person should not be asked to play music so stylistically different. I disagree absolutely! Great players love and revel in all kinds of music, as long as it is good of its kind, in the same way that great actors can give life to all kinds of rôles. Good orchestral and chamber players must be able to produce the widest range of musical interpretations. I would not have it otherwise – it makes musical life so much more interesting. To produce nothing but one style of music for your whole career would be deadly boring!

You may say that I have wandered away from the title of this little essay about teaching, to pursue a few personal hobbyhorses. However, I think not. I am sure that at every stage in teaching, and at every lesson we give, we should have time to instil broader and more stimulating ideas about music in general, and indeed about life in general, to justify our claim that we are aiming at more than training human machines to play perfectly in tune (though that would be nice!). Our ideal should be to spread awareness of the wonderful life-enhancing thing that is there to be grasped by anyone, at any level of achievement playing a musical instrument – and particularly in playing in ensembles. But also, we must remind people that in this life you never get anything for nothing. There is no such thing as a free lunch! Therefore, any pleasure you get from music must be paid for by commitment and hard work. The bonus on offer is that the hard work eventually becomes a pleasure in itself. Kids often don't like practice – I can clearly remember being sent into the front room to do my practice hour. Knowing that my mum would be happy if she could hear me playing away in the distance, I would mindlessly go through scales, studies and pieces that I already could rattle off from memory, and on my music stand would be the "*Hotspu*r" comic! But later, with a few deadlines to meet in the shape of challenging concerts and exams, practice gradually became something I valued finding time for.

There is another reported remark by Mozart that encapsulates much of what I have been saying. He was playing with a cellist, who eventually exclaimed to him – "Oh, it is so unfair! I have to work so hard to play this music and you make it all sound so easy." To which Mozart replied – "I have worked very hard in the past to make it easy now".

So far, I have been discussing violin playing almost entirely from the standpoint of technique. It is obviously important to help and encourage students to gain and to maintain the highest possible level in this respect, but we must never lose sight of the fact that once you begin to bore people you have lost them. If you drone on and on about nothing more than technique, the more intelligent of your students will just lose interest, and those who are more dutiful and faithful to you will become limited in their approach. I am always mindful of the excellent ideas put forward by Ivan Galamian. He suggests that teaching and practice should always be conducted on three levels.

On one level, there are the actual details of how to play, how to use the violin technically and how to exercise and develop the physique needed. This can be equated with the use of exercises, scales and arpeggios and other purely mechanical considerations. Then there is the application of such skills to musical considerations. Here we come to the value of studies and études, where we are confronted with a piece of music specially written to develop particular technical problems. In this respect, string players are less fortunate than pianists, who have études written by such musical giants as Chopin, Schumann, Brahms and Liszt, whereas we have to do with Kreutzer, Rode, Campagnoli etc, (though we do have the wonderful Caprices of Paganini to strive for). But we must remember that a Caprice or Étude is to be played not as a mere exercise, but is devised to transport a particular technical problem into a musical context. In this respect, I recommend the Rode Caprices, which to my mind are musically rewarding and can stimulate the pupil's musical enjoyment.

The final stage is work on mainstream repertoire, where the student will encounter a constant variation of all the technical problems he or she has previously encountered. It is good to refer back to the technical considerations previously encountered, but now musical ideas are paramount, and practice entails the production of actual fully formed performances.

These three stages can equally be applied to the study of some new piece of repertoire. Firstly, by slow practice and repeated study, we must achieve the ability, both physically and mentally, to surmount the various technical problems of the work.

Secondly, we will practice to be able to play all the passages accurately and in correct tempo. (In my experience, rhythm and tempo are the most commonly neglected aspects of most people's practice.) Then thirdly, we must practice to *perform* the actual music, when we aim to interpret the true meaning of the piece itself, regardless of any technical limitations; just to enjoy it.

It is good to get people into the idea of dividing up their work-time equally into these three segments. Too often, students confine all their work within one or other of these disciplines. You have the industrious, analytical student who loves to be submerged in the technical problems, or the player with some technical fluency, who likes to flash through all his music at a speed slightly in excess of Heifetz. Finally, there is the emotionally over-developed character who loves the actual music, but has a mental block, which prevents him or her from hearing the actual travesties of the inspired performances! I was fortunate enough to have a few lessons with the great virtuoso Henryck Szeryng. He said something that I have always remembered. Others have said the same thing, but coming from him, it had greater resonance. He said – "Most people like to practice only what they can do. Those who have a natural pleasing tone production play only soulful slow movements. People with natural quick facility and co-ordination just rattle through impressive technical passages. Everyone should be encouraged to be less self indulgent, and work more on their particular weaknesses."

Finally, I would like to say, that I have always been opposed to those who would confine teaching to a pre-ordained programme of progression from one topic to another. The teaching of a musical instrument is a personal, one-to-one activity that must be uniquely tailored to the individuals concerned, both teacher and pupil. At the earlier stages, class teaching is often a good thing, being useful in instilling basic principles. Master classes at a later stage can help in relate students to their contemporaries and to the fresh ideas of a different instrumental pedagogue, but the main progress is derived from the intimate relationship between a teacher who can combine sympathy and authority, and a pupil who can feel respect and trust. Both sides must contribute, and both must be able to vary the input into this very special and intellectually intimate relationship.

It may be argued that insistence on a dedicated approach by pupils will put many young people off learning an instrument. I don't think this is altogether a bad thing! Very often, children waste much effort in pursuing music studies long after it is obvious that they show no aptitude or love for the subject. Nevertheless, I feel sure that everyone has the ability to take part in some worthwhile activity. Parents and teachers should try to make sure that children are encouraged to explore a range of activities to find what really turns them on. If music does not appeal, try something else.

This does not by any means imply that as teachers we should only accept the highly talented pupils destined to become professional performers. The only reason to do music at all is to get pleasure out of it, and in the end, you only get this pleasure if you attain a reasonable degree of proficiency, but you don't need to be a genius! Many string players have tremendous fun playing their instruments, though they will never be able to play professionally. That is fine! I would never turn away a dedicated amateur. It is they who compose the best part of our audiences; in the world of music, audiences are just as important as players.

Glossop March 30th 2007

Appendix II –
Singing Sound

This article appeared in the June 2008 issue of "News & Views", the journal of the European String Teachers' Association, British Branch.

I can distinctly remember my first lesson in about 1947 with my greatest teacher by far – Sascha Lasserson. I was 24 years old, just out of the Forces, and dead keen to establish myself on the London musical scene, extend my repertoire, improve technically, and prepared to work hard.

Sascha wasn't one of those teachers whose aim when starting a new student is to dismantle their whole apparatus; take them back to square one as it were, and insist on six months of open strings, scales and Ševčik studies, then slowly begin to reconstruct the technique into an exact copy of their own. He accepted people as they were, and proceeded to build on the positive aspects of their ability, talent and character. But he did have a few basic requirements which he recommended, and these I remember from that first encounter. They are things I have taught all my own students ever since.

At that first lesson, after I had played some of the Mendelssohn concerto for him to assess my general standard, he suggested that at the next lesson we should begin work on the Glazunov Concerto, a great favourite of his which he played superbly, in the tradition handed down to him by Auer. But as a starter, he gave me these requirements for daily practice.

First there were scales and arpeggios – a routine to be a regular part of practice sessions. Then, specifically to improve intonation, a simple exercise in building double-stops thirds, based on the scale of C major. This is immensely beneficial and I have used it ever since. It involves very slow practice, absolutely no vibrato, and critical attention to correctness and consistency of intonation.

Then finally we came to the right arm and the bowing technique.

Many people when questioned about string playing will acknowledge freely that the use of the bow is the most important aspect of technique, governing as it does the kind of impact that the bow hairs make on the string, thus being the main ingredient (more even than vibrato) of the kind of sound we make. But, in actual fact, they often do very little specific practice in this respect and sometimes fail to understand the basic principles involved. Sascha's first exercise (if you can call it such) was simply to play long slow open strings with the bow hair quite close to the bridge and with a constant even weight of contact on the string, appreciating that less than the actual weight of the bow is needed near the heel, and that from about the middle to the point, increasing pressure must be applied by the right hand forefinger, assisted by the counter-pressure of the thumb. The tone must be smooth, constant (no cheating!) and as slow as possible. Sascha could make a bow last one entire minute, with a lovely continuous sound throughout – I never managed that! And the change to the next up bow must be smooth and inaudible with absolutely no gap.

Then there were several variations on this.

- Starting *piano* at the heel with gradual crescendo to *forte* at the point and return on the up bow with a diminuendo to *piano* at the heel.

Further Scrapings

- The reverse – starting *forte* at the heel and diminuendo to *piano* at the point, then an up bow crescendo to the heel

- Starting *piano* at the heel with gradual crescendo to *forte* at the middle, then diminuendo to *piano* at the point, and the same dynamics in the following up bow.

- Again the reverse - *forte* at the heel with gradual decrescendo to *piano* at the middle, then crescendo to forte at the point, and the same dynamics in the following up bow.

- Be sure to do several bows on each exercise, so that you also practice an imperceptible bow-change not only at the point but also at the heel, which is more difficult.

- It is also important to realise that in the changes of dynamics, the bow hair must be closer to the bridge for *forte* and nearer the fingerboard for *piano*.

Sascha suggested doing this on all four strings. Maybe in order not to take up too much time, you could choose a different string each day. I have found it also most valuable to practice the slow bows using two strings at once, thus increasing control of the up and down movement of the bow, and ensuring that each string sounds equally clearly.

Practised regularly and conscientiously for ten or fifteen minutes a day, this is guaranteed to increase control of sound quality and dynamics in all parts of the bow. Ideally we must be able to produce whatever volume or quality we like in any part of the bow stroke, whether down or up. Make yourself master of the bow, rather than the bow being your master!

I am pretty sure that many players and indeed many teachers do not pay sufficient attention to this aspect of playing, and I think it is worthwhile to give it some thought. Let us take a clue from the title of this article and study the example of singers and singing teachers. I know that singers regularly practice long slow notes, in all the various registers and in all the different dynamics. The sound of a singer is everything. They realise this and they work on it – so should we. Alfredo Campoli (one of my idols) used to tell me that as soon as he developed his technique (precociously early in his case) his father who was his teacher, got him to listen to all the records of the operatic stars of years gone by. All the truly great string players, and I certainly include Campoli in this category, have a personal sound which may to some extent be due to the character and use of vibrato, but over and above this is due to their control of the bow's movement and weight, which has been carefully studied and controlled. Today I have just read a critique of Leonidas Kavakos, to my mind one of our very finest present day players, in the Nielson Violin Concerto with the LSO and Osmo Vänskä. The critic was John Allison, and I hope he will not mind if I quote –

"Playing the long and demanding work from memory, Kavakos delivered virtuosity and dream-like serenity in equal measure. *He spun lines of shining tone,* (my italics) and in partnership with Vänskä showed what is special about this concerto".

Why is it that I find when listening to so many of our eminent soloists and chamber musicians, the phrase *"lines of shining tone"* so seldom come to mind? It is not the instruments that are lacking. Many have excellent examples of Stradivarius, Guarnerius and so on, and most produce moments of extreme tonal beauty. But too many, even those often highly praised, tend to lack the quality of *line* in their playing. They allow the sound to *dip* as it were. The end of the bow fades away and the whole effect becomes breathy and mannered. Not only that, they are often covered by the orchestra, only emerging every now and then, like sunshine on a cloudy day. This does not happen with Menuhin, Heifetz, Stern, Milstein, any of a host of our violinistic gods, who knew consciously how to spin out that magical line. Sascha knew it, and he also knew how to try to impart it by practical means to his students.

I have thought quite a bit about this since having retired as a player and having the chance to attend more concerts, and my ideas may cause consternation in some quarters. To be concise and direct, I attribute this recent lack of line to the increasing awareness by players of Baroque string style – admirable in itself, but not when applied to Tchaikovsky!

Consider this for a moment. The bow is not a perfect instrument. Down bows and up bows tend to sound different. It is heavy at the heel and lighter at the point. Changes of bow, if not done very skilfully, often disturb the line of the music. Many good composers realise this; for instance Richard Strauss often puts long phrase marks in his string parts and some people think this ignorance of bowing from one who was not a string player. Not so; these are phrase marks, and he leaves it to the expert player to organize his bowing so that it will give effect to them.

In this respect, wind players have the better of us. The breath of an oboist will far outlast the most skilful long bow on the violin, so they are more easily able to present seamless long phrases. I noticed very strongly in a recent performance of Tschaikovsky's Fourth Symphony that the wind phrasing when answering the same figure from the strings, sounded much more linear and convincing, while the strings often sounded rather gusty – again lacking line. We should study wind soloists and try to emulate them.

Think a little of the history of the violin. It emerged in the mid 16th Century; its precursor was probably the Rebec, a three-stringed bowed instrument used for accompanying dancing, folk songs and general festive occasions, and the early violin continued in this role – an instrument for the people rather than the stately viol favoured by the upper classes. The bow would generally be a short "fiddlestick", ideal for quick merry music with lots of marked rhythm. Very few if any have survived from those days – bows were probably then regarded as expendable. Eventually there was the elevation of the instrument into a serious musical tool. With the rise of opera, composers such as Claudio Monteverdi (born in Cremona and a violinist himself) began to appreciate the string family as a perfect "backing" to the human voice, and eventually the ensemble of two violins, viola, cello and bass became probably the most important part of European musical tradition for the next three or four centuries.

But, the short, light-weight bow, often very elegant, and ideal for much of the Italian and French music of the time, mostly written for the sophisticated entertainment of the aristocracy, survived. Composers, who more often than not were themselves violinists, wrote music that suited the nimble and cheerful characteristics of the bow, with brilliant passagework generally in separate bows and the pulse aided by what Leopold Mozart in his Violin Playing calls the "rule of the down bow".

However, this "fiddling" tradition found its limitations when composers began to produce more serious and expressive repertoire. It is known that violinists such as Tartini and Veracini used a longer "solo" bow for music where sustained phrasing was called for. To cut a very long and detailed story short, we come to the end of the 18th century and the beginning of the 19th. It was a time of great change – the French Revolution, Beethoven stretching the boundaries of music far beyond the early fortepianos, larger halls and bigger ensembles, leading to basic changes in the violin – stronger bass-bars, different neck, and greater tension on the strings.

In Paris, the great violinists of the day, Baillot, Kreutzer, Rode etc. all played in the Paris Opera orchestra. Some of them married opera singers. They were influenced by the singing voice and longed to match it. Francois Tourte (the Stradivari of the bow) with the collaboration of Viotti, produced the bow design which met the needs of the times, and which has continued in use practically unchanged ever since. This new bow, as we all know, has a tip with a generous weight of wood, enabling us to retain the agility, bounce and rhythmic vitality of older models, but with increased cohesion to the string, making expressive long phrasing much easier to obtain.

We have moved at a stroke from the Dancing Violin to the Singing Violin. Paganini belongs without doubt to the second category. His music, in spite of the incredible technical fireworks is essentially operatic in character, with beautiful vocal melodies, decorated with the most fantastic *coloratura,* needing every ultimate possibility offered by the new Tourte bow. Could one imagine playing the Beethoven Concerto with an old Corelli type stick? The idea is laughable. A new era of big, expressive string playing began. It still took an expert player to produce long seamless lines, but it was now much more possible.

However, in the later 20th century, musicians became dissatisfied at the way string players, raised in the tradition of late classical, romantic and contemporary music, were playing the masterpieces of the Baroque - Bach, Handel Vivaldi and many others - with heavy, romanticised style, quite inappropriate to the knowledge which was emerging from writings of people like Quantz and CPE Bach. This trend, unfortunately, did at times become something of a band-wagon, with more and more people outdoing each other in the latest fashion of 18th century reconstructed performances, all of course backed up with detailed musicological research! I recently heard a performance of Bach Violin Concerto in E, in which the first three crotchet notes were played absolutely *staccatissmo* with three brutal down bows at the heel. Every following crotchet and quaver was also staccato. It sounded quite grotesque. I am certain that Bach himself would have been outraged. I can only remind myself in cases like that, of the wise words of Bach's most famous son Carl Philip Emanuel - "The only ultimate arbiter in judging musical performance is good taste."

Fortunately, such monstrosities and exaggerations are comparatively rare, and it is usual nowadays to hear stylish, excellent playing of Baroque and early Classical music from the many chamber orchestras around, whether they be playing with modern instruments and bows, or they are what some of my colleagues refer to as "oldy worldy" experts – gut strings and no chinrests allowed!. The bowing is springy and lively – quavers have a nice firm attack, and are generally sounded with a sensitive diminuendo which gives a stylish bell-like quality to the notes. The point of the bow is used for *piano,* the heel for *forte,* up bows for crescendo and down bows for emphasis. In fact, the bow is allowed to do just what comes naturally to it.

Unfortunately, in music from about the last two hundred years, composers have asked us to do much more than this. We often hear the complaint from players that some music is not "violinistic", but the greatest composers, from Beethoven onwards, often are unable to limit their imagination for our benefit, and we have to develop our technique to cope with these demands.

I feel that in recent years, the admirable and successful attempts to play Baroque music with style and grace, have led to this kind of playing as it were leaking over into general performance. I would like to see and hear more body in the tone, more shaping of longer phrases, more imaginative use of the bow to create the continuity of sound and the projection needed for today's concert halls. Fill out the sound of long notes for their entire length, like a great singer. For this to be so, I must reiterate what has been said earlier, we must not let the bow be our master – we must master the bow.

18/12/2007

Index

A

Academy of the BBC vii, 190, 192
Aikieslack 51, 53
Albert Hall 30, 84, 86, 142
Alexander, Fred 115
Alhambra Theatre 41
Allison, John 214
Anda, Geza 185
Ansermiére, Nellie 80
Apollo Theatre 115, 117
Armon, William (Bill Tilley) 68
Arts Council 109, 110, 111, 226
Associated Board 11, 44
Atkinson, John (Morava) 15, 18

B

Bach 14, 21, 67, 80, 81, 112, 115, 132, 141, 177, 184, 217, 225
Baines, Francis 69
Baker, Richard 196
Barbirolli, John 18, 36, 71, 132, 140, 179
Barenboim, Daniel 178
Barker, Alfred 129, 138
Bartok, Bela 84
Bax 69, 70, 81
BBC Maida Vale 120
BBC Scottish Orchestra 79
BBC Symphony Orchestra 85, 129, 140, 141, 143
BBC Training Orchestra vii, 73, 81, 92, 138, 170, 188
Bean, Hugh 139
Beard, Paul 129, 140, 141, 142, 143
Beecham, Thomas 18, 23, 24, 92, 129, 138, 140, 178, 180, 227
Beethoven 30, 46, 70, 85, 105, 112, 120, 133, 140, 177, 186, 192, 206, 216, 217, 218

Bentley, Douglas 20, 21
Berg, Alban 3
Berlin Wall 164
Berlioz, Hector 105, 177
Bingley Grammar School 9, 26
Bizet Symphony 193, 194
Blech, Harry 92, 93
Blitz 54, 64, 73, 88
Bloch, Alexander 199
Bloch, Joe 78
Bor, Edward (Teddy) 71
Bor, Hilda 71
Bor, Sam 71
Bor, Sylvia 71
Boskovsky, Willie 147, 148
Boulanger, Nadia 99
Boult, Adrian 18, 81, 129, 178, 195, 196
Boyd Neel Chamber Ensemble 69
Boyd Neel Orchestra vii, 67, 69, 82, 92, 93, 97, 169
Brahms 19, 21, 72, 114, 132, 139, 146, 186, 208, 226, 227
Brain, Aubrey 225
Brain, Dennis 92, 109, 127, 225
Britten, Benjamin 69, 81, 99, 109, 191
Buckman, Rosina 76
Bulow, Hans von 178
Bush 140

C

Cameron, Douglas 71
Campoli 121, 214
Cantelli, Guido 14, 178, 179
Carpenter, Norman 51
Catteral, Arthur 77
CEMA 110
Chadwick, Bob 171
Chamberlain, Neville 52
Chaplin, Charles 49
Child, Les 189
Churchill, Winston 50, 52, 90, 164, 227
Clarke, Raymond 21, 23

Coates, Albert 18, 76
Coates, Tamara 76
Cohen, Harriet 16, 139
Collier, Derek 104
Collinson's Tea Rooms 23
Colston Hall 23, 189, 191, 194
Communist 112, 113, 185
Concertmaster 139, 227
Constantine, Norman 23
Copperwheat, Winifred 81
Cordell, Doreen 81
Cordell, Joyce 72, 73, 81
Coronation 99, 164
Cosma, Edgar 193, 195
County Major Scholarship 31
Coventry 75, 98, 191
Craxton, Harold 16
Cuban Missile Crisis 164
Curwen, Mrs 10
Curzon, Clifford 16, 148

D

D'Oisley, Maurice 76, 140
Dalbeattie 51, 53
Dale, Muriel (Angela) v, 70, 111
Dart, Thurston 67
Dartington 66, 81
Datyner, Henry 165
David, Ferdinand 134
Davies, Meredith 125, 191
Davis, Colin 178, 180
Davison, Arthur 102
Davison, Doris 83
Delius 21, 46, 144, 191, 192
Disney 52
Dixon, Ivy 72
Dohnanyi 225
Dorabella 226
Douglas, Keith 22, 23
Drake, Edgar 19
Draper, Mendelssohn 15, 24, 31, 134, 139, 148, 177, 211, 225
Dunkirk 53
Dunn, John 35
Dutton, Walter 13, 14

E

Eastbrook Hall 24
ECO 190
Eden, Mollie 70
Eggleton, Betty 70
Elgar, Edward 30, 39, 69, 133, 139, 145, 195, 226
Elstree 116, 145
English Chamber Orchestra 68, 99
Eric Greene 225
Essex, Kenneth 67
Everest 12, 99, 164, 192

F

Ferrier, Kathleen 109
Festival of Britain 109, 164
Fields, Gracie 7, 50
Fleming, Amaryllis 67
Flesch, Carl 37, 144, 199, 206
Fletcher, Lynn 129
Foldes, Andor 185
Francis, John 122
Franco 49, 52
Friend, Rodney 37
Furtwangler, Wilhelm 178

G

Galamian, Ivan 207
Gamba, Pierino 186
Gauntlett, Ambrose 139
Geiger, Hans 103, 104, 145
George V 48
Gershwin, George 3, 4
Gestapo 94
Gilbert, Max 82, 92, 93
Glazunov 183, 211
Glock, William 188, 189, 196
Glyndebourne 139, 183, 188
Godowsky, Leopold 226
Goldwyn, Sam 95
Goosens, Leon 69
Green, Rosemary 69, 82
Griller String Quartet 92

Grinke, Fred 92, 93, 97, 119
Groves, Charles 133, 178
Guarnerius 34, 81, 214
Gunn, Neil 76

H

Hall, Joy 71
Hallé Orchestra 18, 22, 36
Halling, Pat 67, 69
Halling, Peter 71
Hall Barrie 165
Hampstead 64, 69, 100, 103, 141
Handel 18, 38, 46, 78, 108, 196, 217
Handel, Ida 78, 108
Harewood, Lord 105
Hartley, Fred 182
Harty, Hamilton 18, 138, 139
Heath, Edward 196
Heath, Ted 119
Hedges, Joyce 73
Hegedus, Olga 111
Heifetz, Jascha 38, 39, 136, 140, 146, 209, 214, 226
Hess, Myra 16, 88, 115
Hiawatha 30, 31
Hill, Judy 111, 121
Hill, Naomi 33
Hinchliffe, Jessie 104, 145, 198
Hirsch, Leonard 92, 93, 138, 188
Hitler, Adolf 2, 29, 52, 53, 65
Hi Gang 118
Hockney, David 12
Hollywood 46, 50, 95, 116
Holmes, Jack 119
Holst, Imogen 99
Hooper, Charles 31
Hooton, Florence 93
Hoyle, Fred 27, 28, 31
Hubicki, Bohdan 73
Hubicki, Peggy 73
Huddersfield Technical College 23
Hungarian Revolution 185
Hurst, George 178, 192
Hurwitz, Manny 68, 78, 192
Hylton, Jack 182

I

Ilkley Concert Club 111
Irving, Ernest 83
Isherwood, Cherry 165

J

Jeans, Sir James 40
Jenkins, Rae 8, 121
Jones, Granville 66, 186
Jowett 103, 104, 106
Jullien, Louis Antoine 177

K

Karajan 21, 104, 105, 106, 178
Karloff, Boris 116
Kavakos, Leonidas 214
Kaye, Arthur Willie 16, 28, 35, 36, 37, 198, 199
Kempe, Rudolf 178, 180
Kennedy, John 72
Kennedy, Nigel 72
Kersey, Eda 80
Kessler, Jack 104, 145, 146
Kirkland, John 77, 78, 82, 120, 140
Klemperer. Otto 21, 135, 140, 178
Kletzki, Paul 178, 228
Kodak 49
Kok, Felix 66
Korean War 164
Kreisler, Fritz 24, 38, 133, 140, 141, 205
Krips, Josef 227
Kurtz, Efrem 183, 184

L

Lampe, Oscar 115
Lasserson, Sascha 97, 201, 202, 211
Lauland, Jürgen 69
Lavers, Marjorie 81
Lee Bernard 116, 117
Legge, Walter 93, 104, 109, 200
Leipzig Gewandhaus Orchestra 134
Lempfert, Marjorie (Bunty) 82

Lenin 2
Leonard, Lawrence (Frankie) 71
Ley, Margie 72
Liverpool Walker Art Gallery 148
Lockyer, James 82
London Harpsichord Ensemble 122
London Mozart Players 93
Lowendall 34, 79
LPO 37, 86, 97, 144, 188
LSO 67, 86, 97, 118, 139, 183, 186, 196, 214

M

MacDonald, Gerald (Gerry) 72
MacDonald, Margaret 75
Mackie, Jean 73, 167
Macmillan 164
Macpherson, Stewart 50
Mahler, Gustav 31, 109, 227
Mahoney, Gilbert 13
Mannes, Leopold 226
Mantovani 112, 140, 141, 182
Mar, Norman Del 92, 178, 180, 191
Marchant, Sir Stanley 67
Martin, David 92
Martin, Irene 16
Matthay, Tobias 16, 198
Matthews, Thomas 129, 144
Matthews Dennis 92, 93
Maude, Edward 18
McCallum, David 18
McMahon, Ivor 68
Medland, H.M. 95
Mendelssohn 15, 24, 31, 134, 139, 148, 177, 211, 225
Menuhin, Yehudi 73, 184, 214
Merret, James 93
Miller, Niven 99
Milner, Martin 133
Milstein, Nathan 148, 214
Moeran 70, 140
Monopoly 49
Monsewer Eddie Gray 41
Monteux, Pierre 178
Monteverdi, Claudio 216

Montgomery 90
Moore, Philip 188, 195, 196
Morecambe and Wise 68
Mountain, Frank 33
Mountain, Frederick 10, 33
Mountain, Grandma (Naomi) 5, 7, 9, 12, 27
Mountain, Harry 4, 33
Mozart 30, 39, 40, 69, 93, 130, 148, 204, 205, 207, 216
Mozart, Leopold 204, 216

P

Paganini 78, 113, 208, 217
Paley, John 19
Parikian, Manoug 127, 145
Pearson, Jeanette 72
Perlman, Itzakh 37
Philharmonia Orchestra 14
Philomusica 66
Popperwell, Stanley 69, 82
Pougnet, Jean 144
Poulenc 194
Previn, Andre 68, 182
Princes Theatre 41
Pritchard, John 122, 133, 135, 178, 183, 184
Purcell 69

Q

Queens Hall 84, 140

R

Rabin, Michael 200
Rankl, Karl 129
Rawsthorne, Alan 198
Reiner, Fritz 178
Renault 99, 103
Rennie, Jean 129
Ricci, Ruggiero 186, 204
Ricketts, Kenneth 93, 95
Riddell, Joyce 73
Rignold, Hugo 182, 183
Robinson, Hilary 69

Robjohns, Sydney 68, 69, 78
Rogerson, Haydn 21
Roosevelt 52, 89
Rosé, Arnold 147, 227, 228
Rostal, Max 85
Rowlette, Tom 142
Royal Academy of Music 18, 31, 40, 54, 64, 121, 182
Royal Liverpool Philharmonic Orchestra vii, 24, 132
Royal Marines 64, 83, 88, 92, 93
Royal Marine Band vii, 93
Royal Philharmonic Society 23
Royal Scottish Academy of Music 197
RPO 72, 118
Rufer, Josef 3, 225
Ruggerius 79
Russell Bertrand 8
Ruth Railton 73

S

Salt, Sir Titus 11
Saltaire 11, 12, 14
Sammons, Albert 138, 139, 140
Sarasate, Pablo de 121, 206
Sargent, Malcolm 18, 19, 30, 140, 178, 182
Sauer, Colin 22, 66, 80
Schoenberg, Arnold 2, 3, 225
School of Music 23, 24, 93, 226
Scott, Ernest 67, 69, 104
Scottish National Orchestra 86
Semino, Norino 81
Šev_ik, Otokar 15, 35, 198
Shaw, George Bernard 40
Shiner, Ronald 115, 116, 117
Sibelius 84, 183
Siki, Bela 185
Silver, Millicent 12, 122
Simpson, Robert 121
Smith, Ronald 71
Somogyi, László 186
Sons, Maurice 140
Spohr, Ludwig 177

Stalin 2
Stokowski, Leopold 178, 188
Stoner, Lieutenant 95
Stoner, Priscilla 72
Stradivarius 79, 80, 214
Stratton, George 139
Strauss, Richard 86, 92, 130, 143, 145, 148, 192, 215, 227
Strinasacchi, Regina 130
St George's Hall 24
Suez Crisis 164
Sunday Observance Society 23
Susskind, Walter 178, 193
Sutcliffe, Jock 105
Sydney Clarke 23
Székely, Josef 84
Szell, George 86
Szeryng, Henryck 132, 209
Szigeti, Josef 146, 227

T

Talbot 101, 102, 103
Tippett, Michael 194, 195
Toscanini, Arturo 31, 93, 140, 178, 179
Tresehar, Daidy 82, 83
Truman 164
Tschaikovsky 89, 215
Turner, Laurence 21, 133, 198
Tzipine, Georges 187

V

Vasary, Tamas 185
Vienna Philharmonic Orchestra 130, 147, 227

W

Wagner, Richard 39, 118, 171, 177
Walenn, Herbert 70, 71
Walton, William 135, 136, 191
Wamsley 35
Watson, Harry 21
Webern, Anton von 3
Whitehead, James 92, 93

Wilhelmji 201
Williams, Vaughan 109, 142, 195
Wilson, Marie 104, 129, 134, 143
Withers, Jane 104
Wood, Dorothy 4
Wood, Grandpa 6
Wood, Henry 78, 86, 89, 178
Woodhouse, Francesca 79
Woof, Rowsby 32, 66, 68, 69, 73, 79, 80, 82, 85, 92, 142, 144, 201, 204

Y

Yorkshire Dales 9, 51
Yorkshire Symphony Orchestra 18
Yugoslavia 112

Z

Zorian, Olive 81

(Footnotes)

[1] Josef Rufer, a student of Schoenberg's intermittently from 1919 through to 1929, compiled the first and still most comprehensive list and description of Schoenberg's music, text, and art works.

[2] Twelve-tone system, in other words twelve equal semitones.

[3] On a recent first visit to Australia to celebrate the fifth birthday of my first great-grandchild, I was taken to the beautiful Royal Botanical Gardens in Sydney for a lovely view over to Sydney Harbour Bridge. Walking through this beautiful park, I was fascinated to see that white cockatoos exactly like Billy which are exotic specimens here in Britain were present in great flocks, almost like the pigeons in our own parks.

[4] Her teacher was a member of a well-known family of woodwind players, Mendelssohn Draper. He was best known as a bass-clarinet player, and often played in chamber ensembles with the hornist Aubrey Brain, father of the great Dennis Brain. He was also an example of the 19th century predilection in musical families of giving their offspring the names of great composers. The mind boggles at the thought of a poor little schoolboy being burdened with the unwieldy first name of Mendelssohn!

[5] This included our first performance of the Sonata in C sharp minor by the Hungarian composer Ernst von Dohnanyi, which became a great favourite of ours and which we later recorded for the BBC. Regrettably this fine work has been inexplicably neglected by most violinists. It is one of the composer's most successful chamber works and is also a brilliant showpiece for both players.

[6] This culminated in meeting at the Royal Academy my future wife, Muriel Dale, who was over four years my senior.

[7] Northern musical audiences can be equally hard to win over, though they sometimes temper their criticism with a modicum of kindness. The story was told to me by the tenor Eric Greene, famous in his time as Evangelist in the Bach Passions. He was on the Huddersfield railway station platform the morning after a St Matthew performance at the Town Hall, awaiting his train back to London. A man in uniform, probably the station master, accosted him.

"O 'ello, I 'eard your concert last night.

"O, good – did you enjoy it?"

"Nay, A thowt it were rubbish. Mind you, A doan't blame thee. A blame 'im as sent thee!"

[8] Kodachrome was invented by two American musicians, Leopold Godowsky Jnr, and Leopold Mannes. As young men, they did their early experimental work in the kitchens and bathrooms of their parents' houses. Apparently they timed the exposures and development baths in complete darkness by humming the last movement of Brahms First Symphony. Because of their names, people said that this highly successful process came from God and Man.

In later life, Godowsky, a violinist, went on to play chamber music with Heifetz, and Mannes became Principal of the Mannes School of Music, New York, which had been founded by his father.

[9] Council for the Encouragement of Music and the Arts – later to evolve into the Arts Council of Great Britain.

[10] Fixers are the orchestral managers who hire players as deputies in the main orchestras or for sessions and other free-lance work,

[11] Nowadays everybody talks about "Gigs". I *hate* that term – it seems to me cheap and nasty! I prefer "dates"

[12] That concert was made memorable to us when we met the President of the Club, a very elderly lady called Dora Penny, and we realised that we were talking to "Dorabella", Elgar's inspiration for Variation 10 (Intermezzo: Allegretto) " of the Enigma Variations. She was one of the "friends pictured within" whose stutter (or laugh, depending on the source) is depicted by the woodwinds. Dora was the stepdaughter of the sister of William Meath Baker, inspiration for the fourth variation, and sister-in-law of Richard Baxter Townsend, inspiration for the third. She was also the recipient of another of Elgar's enigmas, the so-called Dorabella Cipher

[13] My home town is of course Shipley, but it is a mere three miles from Bradford, and has for many years been part of Bradford Metropolitan District.

[14] There was a visit to the London Coliseum Theatre by a group called the Italian International Opera Company, giving a fortnight of varied popular repertoire. One critic reviewed their efforts as follows (I quote from memory) - "In England we look to Italy as the land of great opera and supreme operatic voices. Sometimes we must remind ourselves that here we generally only encounter the cream of this national product, and realise that to produce a small amount of cream it requires a large amount of milk. It must be said that the singers of the Italian International Opera Company are not the cream of their country's artists: they are not even the milk – they would better be described as the whey!"

[15] He married Winston Churchill's daughter, Sarah, in 1936, but was divorced in 1945.There is an anecdote, possibly apocryphal, that Oliver once asked his father-in-law (who loathed him) who was the most impressive figure in the war. Churchill replied, "Mussolini." When asked why, the former prime minister supposedly replied, "Because he shot his son-in-law!"

[16] "Sir Thomas Beecham – A Centenary Tribute" – Macdonald and Janes – London 1979

[17] She was god-mother to our second baby, Alison, and entertained her lavishly. When Alison had a 4th birthday, Marie took her out to Madame Tussauds, and a lovely tea in Baker Street. Coming home was rush hour, so Marie, no expense spared, hailed a taxi. This was a new experience for Alison whose only private transport up to then had been the family car. They settled comfortably in the back, and Alison whispered to Marie, pointing cautiously at the driver – "Is that your Daddy?"

[18] Josef Krips is a conductor whom I have previously and unaccountably failed to mention. I only played under him a few times, but this was enough to realise that he was a person of immense musical magnetism. One writer described him well as a "benevolent despot". He was a corpulent man, with big blue eyes which at moments of musical climax would open into large glowing orbs. One such moment I remember was the entry of the trombones in the last movement of Brahms 4th Symphony – what incredible tension he created. He could be quite threatening, though. We were recording some Viennese items with him once in Abbey Road Studios, and began the Fledermaus Overture of Strauss. The brilliant upward flourish of violins half way down the first page was not to his satisfaction, even after a second attempt. "Very vell" he snarled in a menacing Teutonic accent "eef it iss not bettah ze next time, I weel heer effery first wiolin separately!!" It sounded like a Nazi Gauleiter threatening to shoot all the hostages. Not unexpectedly, the next attempt was impeccably note-perfect!

[19] This is shown particularly in Szigeti's arrangement for violin and piano of "Capriol Suite" by Peter Warlock.

[20] One of these was in Glasgow, and it was the only time that I have ever performed in the old St Andrew's Hall, famous for having perhaps the best acoustical qualities in Britain. That was in 1962, and within a few weeks of our concert it was completely destroyed in a disastrous fire.

[21] Arnold Rosé (born Rosenblum, 1863-1946, the Romanian-born Austrian Jewish violinist was leader of the Vienna Philharmonic Orchestra for over half a century. He worked closely with Brahms and Gustav Mahler was his brother-in-law. Although not known internationally as a soloist he was a great orchestral leader (concertmaster) and player of chamber music, leading the famous Rosé String

Quartet for several decades. Rose was a fugitive from Nazi persecution in 1938, subsequently living in St John's Wood, London. When I was a student there during the War, he was pointed out to me in the street though I never met him.

[22] Paul Kletzki, Polish conductor and composer, born in Lodz 1900. Trained as a violinist. In March 1973, after I had left Liverpool, he finally did manage to get to the city for a date as guest conductor on 5th March, but tragically died in the Green Room, in the interval of the rehearsal.

Printed in the United Kingdom
by Lightning Source UK Ltd.
132966UK00002B/196-294/P